PAINT SHOP PRO
in easy steps

Stephen Copestake

COMPUTER
STEP

In easy steps is an imprint of Computer Step
Southfield Road . Southam
Warwickshire CV33 OFB . England

Tel: 01926 817999 Fax: 01926 817005
http://www.computerstep.com

Notice of Liability
Every effort has been made to ensure that this book contains accurate
and current information. However, Computer Step and the author shall
not be liable for any loss or damage suffered by readers as a result of
any information contained herein.

Trademarks
All trademarks are acknowledged as belonging to their respective
companies.

Printed and bound in the United Kingdom

ISBN 1-874029-95-4

Contents

3   Painting/drawing   59

4   Using filters   95

5 Deformations and effects   139

6 Advanced techniques   169

Index   **189**

First steps

In this chapter, you'll learn how to use the Paint Shop Pro screen; create new files; open existing ones; and save changes to disk. You'll rescale images, and resize the underlying canvas. You'll also learn about image formats, then use special screen modes. You'll zoom in and out on images, and reverse image amendments. Finally, you'll learn how to work with background/foreground colours.

Covers

The Paint Shop Pro screen

Version 3 of Paint Shop Pro has a slightly different screen. Note the following:

- The Style Palette is known as the Tool Control Panel
- The Tool Palette is split into two separate entities: the Select Toolbox and the Paint Toolbox
- There is no Colour Palette

Additionally, the Tool Control Panel, Select Toolbox and Paint Toolbox 'float' on screen (rather than being fixed under the Toolbar).

The Paint Shop Pro screen is exceptionally easy to use. When you run the program, this is the result:

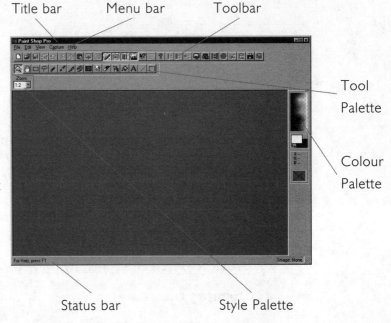

Title bar   Menu bar   Toolbar

Tool Palette

Colour Palette

Status bar   Style Palette

The following are details of screen components specific to Paint Shop Pro:

The Toolbar
This is a collection of icons. By clicking an appropriate icon, you can launch a specific feature.

The other components are common to most or all Windows programs. See your Windows documentation for how to use them.

The Tool Palette
A specialised toolbar which you use to launch a variety of tools (e.g. the Zoom tool – see pages 22-23).

The Colour Palette
An easy and convenient way to access Paint Shop Pro's colour selection tools.

The Style bar
Customises the tool currently selected in the Tool Palette

Customising screen components

You can use two techniques to specify which screen components display:

In version 3, the View menu is slightly different.

The menu route

Pull down the View menu and do the following:

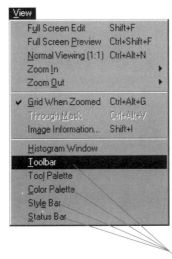

If any of these menu entries has ✔ against it, carrying out step 1 will remove the relevant component from the screen.

Click one of these

The Toolbar route

In version 4 only, refer to the on-screen Toolbar and do the following:

Click here to hide/show the Style bar

Click here to hide/show the Tool Palette

Click here to hide/show the Colour Palette

Opening files

Version 3 supports slightly fewer formats.

Version 4 of Paint Shop Pro will open (i.e. read and display) some 35 separate graphics file formats. These fall into two broad categories: raster and vector – see page 20 for details of some of the principal image formats supported by Paint Shop Pro. When you tell Paint Shop Pro to open an image, it automatically recognises which format it was written to, and acts accordingly. It does this by taking account of the file suffix. For example, TIFF (Tagged Image File Format) images – to be opened in Paint Shop Pro – must end in:

.TIF

Not all of the supported formats, however, can be written to disk. (See page 18 for how to save files.)

Paint Shop Pro also opens images considerably more rapidly than just about any other paint program.

You open files via the Open dialog (the Open Image dialog in version 3 of Paint Shop Pro).

Carry out the following procedures:

Opening images

Pull down the File menu and do the following:

Paint Shop Pro stores details of recently opened files here. To reopen one of these, simply click the relevant entry. (Omit steps 1-3 on page 11).

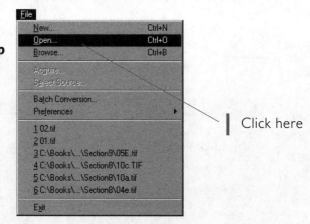

Click here

...contd

Now carry out the following steps:

1 Click here. In the drop-down list, select the relevant drive/folder

Paint Shop Pro version 4 comes with a quantity of prepared images. These can be found in the IMAGES folder on the supplied CD.

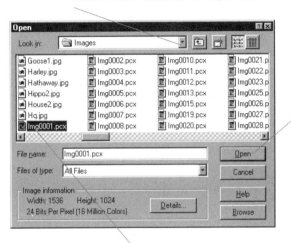

3 Click here

2 Click a graphics file

In version 3, the Open Image dialog launches. This differs from the version 4 dialog. Don't perform steps 1-3; instead, do the following:

Paint Shop Pro now opens the image.

A Select a folder & drive

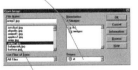

The opened image

B Double-click a file

Resampling/resizing files

Paint Shop Pro lets you change image dimensions in the following ways:

Resizing

When you resize an image, Paint Shop Pro performs permutations of the following (necessarily simplistic) actions:

Pixels (the word is a contraction of 'picture element') are dots, the smallest element which can be displayed on screen.
  Bitmapped graphics consist of pixels; each is allocated a colour (or greyscale).

- pixels are deleted

- pixels are reproduced

to produce the required dimensions.

Resampling

Resampling is a more complex procedure. When you resample an image, Paint Shop Pro performs an interpolation. This simply means that it attempts to predict how pixels between known colours should appear. The result, generally, is a sharper, more focused image, but one which takes slightly longer to generate.

Suggestions for use

Use resizing for images:

— which consist of 16 colours, or fewer

— which are simple (i.e. contain few components)

Enlarging or shrinking bitmaps (whichever of the two methods you use) produces *some* level of distortion.
  The trick is to minimise this as far as possible.

Use resampling for images:

— which are complex (e.g. photographs, or pictures with many components)

— which are greyscale (i.e. the colours have been converted to shades of grey) or have 256 (or more) colours

...contd

Resizing an image

Pull down the Image menu and click Resize. Now carry out
step 1 OR 2 below. Finally, perform step 3:

1 Click a predetermined size

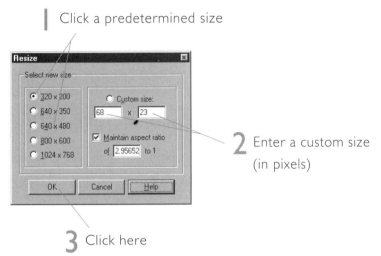

 **As far as
the user is
concerned,
resizing
and resampling are
almost identical
procedures;
however, what
Paint Shop Pro does
behind the scenes
varies enormously.**

2 Enter a custom size
(in pixels)

3 Click here

Resampling an image

Pull down the Image menu and click Resample. Now carry
out step 1 OR 2 below. Finally, perform step 3:

 **Re. step 2
– the box
on the left
represents
width, that on the
right height.**

1 Click a predetermined size

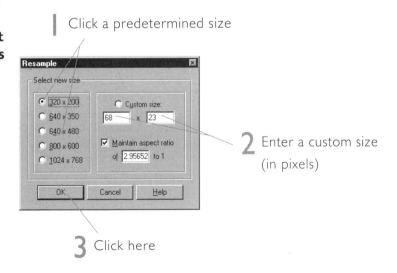

2 Enter a custom size
(in pixels)

3 Click here

New files

Often, images will be 'ready-made' for you, in the sense that you'll:

- open existing images (see pages 10-11)

- create screenshots by carrying out screen captures (see Chapter 6)

- duplicate existing images (see page 15)

However, there will be times when you'll need to create an image from scratch. Paint Shop Pro makes this easy, but there are several stages:

1. launching the New Image dialog

2. specifying the width and height, in pixels

3. selecting an image type (including the number of colours)

4. selecting a background colour

Creating a new image

Pull down the File menu and do the following:

In version 3, the File menu is slightly different.

HANDY TIP

Versions 3 and 4 use different techniques for selecting a background colour. (See page 29 for how to do this.) **Additionally, version 3 users must carry out step 4 on the right** *before* **steps 1-3 (steps 1-3 equate to steps 1-6 on page 15).**

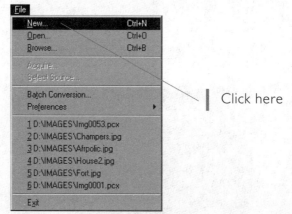

File	
New...	Ctrl+N
Open...	Ctrl+O
Browse...	Ctrl+B
Acquire...	
Select Source...	
Batch Conversion...	
Preferences ▶	
1 D:\IMAGES\Img0053.pcx	
2 D:\IMAGES\Champers.jpg	
3 D:\IMAGES\Afrpolic.jpg	
4 D:\IMAGES\House2.jpg	
5 D:\IMAGES\Fort.jpg	
6 D:\IMAGES\Img0001.pcx	
Exit	

Click here

...contd

Now carry out the following steps:

If, when you follow step 6, you receive this message:

your system has too little memory for the size/type of image you were trying to create. Click OK. Then repeat steps 1-6, but choose smaller dimensions in step 1 and/or fewer colours in steps 4-5.

To duplicate an active image, click its title bar. Pull down the Window menu and click Duplicate; Paint Shop Pro opens the copy in its own (new) window.

1 Type in image dimensions

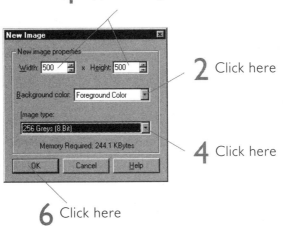

2 Click here

4 Click here

6 Click here

5 Select an image type

The following is the result:

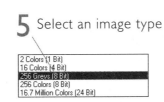

3 Select a background colour

A new (blank) image (the background colour is white) in its own window

Enlarging an image's canvas

 Note that enlarging an image's canvas (unlike resampling/ resizing) does not expand the image itself.

As we've seen on pages 14-15, when you can create an image from scratch, you specify the width and height in pixels. When you do this, Paint Shop Pro automatically defines a 'canvas' (the area on which the image lies) with the same dimensions. However, you can easily specify increased dimensions for the canvas.

When you increase an image's canvas, Paint Shop Pro inserts the active background colour:

- around the image itself (if you carry out step 2 on page 17)

- to the left of and below the image (if you don't carry out step 2 on page 17)

Increasing an image's canvas

First, follow steps 2-4 on page 29 to select a background colour. Then pull down the Image menu and do the following:

 In version 3, the Image menu is slightly different.

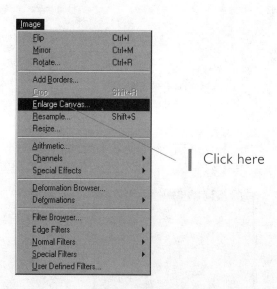

Click here

Now carry out the following steps:

1 Type in revised canvas dimensions

3 Click here

2 Optional – click here to centre the image

See the 'before' and 'after' illustrations below:

An image
and its
original
(identical)
canvas

The same image
centred within
an enlarged
canvas (here,
the background
is white)

Saving files

In version 3, the Save As dialog is slightly different. Do the following:

Select a drive/folder in the Drives and Directories fields. Select a format/sub-format in the List Files of Type and File Sub-Format fields respectively. Name the file in the File Name box. Finally, click OK.

Re. step 2 – many image formats have sub-formats you can choose from.

For example, TIFF (the bitmap format preferred by most page-layout programs) has 6 available sub-formats in Paint Shop Pro, many of which incorporate compression.

When you're working on one or more images in Paint Shop Pro, it's important to save your work at frequent intervals, in order to avoid data loss in the event of a hardware fault or power interruption.

Saving a file for the first time

Pull down the File menu and click Save. Now do the following:

3 Click here. In the drop-down list, click a drive/folder combination

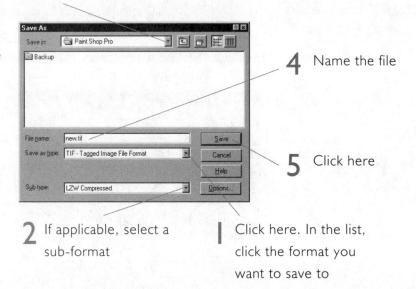

4 Name the file

5 Click here

2 If applicable, select a sub-format

I Click here. In the list, click the format you want to save to

Saving previously saved files

Pull down the File menu and click Save. No dialog launches; instead, Paint Shop Pro saves the latest version of your file to disk, overwriting the previous version.

File formats – an overview

The images Paint Shop Pro works with fall into two broad categories:

- bitmaps

- vector images

Both are defined below.

Bitmap images

Bitmaps consist of pixels (dots) arranged in such a way that they form a graphic image. Because of the very nature of bitmaps, the question of 'resolution' – the sharpness of an image expressed in dpi (dots per inch) – is important. Bitmaps look best if they're displayed at their correct resolution. Paint Shop Pro imports (i.e. translates into its own format) a wide variety of third-party bitmap formats.

Once you've finished working with bitmaps, you can export the finished result as another bitmap. In this way, they can be utilised in other programs (e.g. CorelDRAW).

Vector images

Paint Shop Pro will also import vector graphics files in formats native to other programs. Vector images consist of, and are defined by, algebraic equations. One practical result of this is that they can be rescaled without any loss of definition. Another corollary is that they're less complex than bitmaps: they contain less detail. Vector files can also include bitmap information.

When it imports vectors, Paint Shop Pro converts them to a bitmap format. When it exports bitmaps to formats which can contain both vector and bitmap information (e.g. WMF – see page 20), only bitmap information is written.

Paint Shop Pro will read (but not write) vector files.
  For example, it will read (and convert into its own internal bitmap format) CorelDRAW files (vectors). However, you can't make changes and export (i.e. save) them back into a new CorelDRAW file: you can only export to *bitmap* formats.

Brief notes on image formats

Paint Shop Pro will import a wide selection of bitmap and vector graphic formats. These are some of the main ones:

Bitmap formats

Many bitmap formats have compression as an option. This allows bitmaps – often very large – to be stored on disk in much smaller files.

PCX	Originated with PC Paintbrush. Used for years to transfer graphics data between Windows application. Supports compression.
TIFF	Tagged Image File Format. Suffix: .TIF. If anything, even more widely used than PCX, across a whole range of platforms and applications.
BMP	Not as common as PCX and TIFF, but still popular. Tends to produce large files.
TGA	Targa. A high-end format, and also a bridge with so-called low-end computers (e.g. Amiga and Atari). Often used in PC and Mac paint and ray-tracing programs because of its high-resolution colour fidelity. Supports compression.
GIF	Graphics Interchange Format. Developed for the on-line transmission of graphics data across the CompuServe network. Just about any Windows program - and a lot more besides - will read GIF. Disadvantage: it can't handle more than 256 colours. Compression is supported.
PCD	(Kodak) PhotoCD. Used primarily to store photographs on CD. Paint Shop Pro will only read 24-bit PCD files and won't export to PCD.

Another bitmap format – JPEG (Joint Photographic Experts Group) – is used on the PC and the Mac for photograph storage. It supports an extremely high-level of compression, usually without appreciable distortion.

Vector formats

CGM	Computer Graphics Metafile. Frequently used in the past, especially as a medium for clip-art transmission. Less frequently used nowadays.
WMF	Windows Metafile. Similar to CGM, but even more frequently used. Used for information exchange between just about all Windows programs.

Full Screen Edit mode

Paint Shop Pro has a special screen mode which (temporarily) hides the following screen components:

Version 3 does not have a Full Screen Edit mode. However, it does have the next best thing: a Full Screen mode which you can use to preview images.
  See page 25.

- the Title bar

- the Menu bar

- the Status bar

The result is that you have more space to work in.

Entering Full Screen Edit mode (version 4 only)

Pull down the View menu and click Full Screen Edit.

An image viewed normally

If you want to hide further screen components (e.g. the Toolbar or Tool Palette), follow the procedures on page 9.

To return to normal edit mode, press Shift+F.

An image in Full Screen Edit mode

Zoom

The ability to 'zoom in' (magnify) or 'zoom out' (reduce magnification) is very important when you're working with images in Paint Shop Pro. When you zoom in or out, Paint Shop Pro increases or reduces the magnification by single increments.

This is best demonstrated by examining the following illustrations:

Here, Paint Shop Pro has not increased the size of the containing window in line with the change in magnification.

To have it do so, version 4 users should pull down the File menu and click Preferences, General Program Preferences. Select the Viewing tab. Click either or both fields in the Zooming section. Click OK.

Version 3 users, on the other hand, should pull down the File menu and click Preferences, General. Select the General tab. Click Fit Window to Image When Zooming. Click OK.

An image – at its original magnification

The same image – magnified by one increment

The same image – with the magnification reduced by one increment

...contd

Zooming in and out (in version 4)

Refer to the Tool Palette and do the following:

Click here

To zoom in or out in version 3 of Paint Shop Pro, refer to the Select Toolbox and do the following:

The mouse pointer changes to a magnifying glass; move this over the part of the image you want to zoom in or out on:

Click here

Now follow the procedures on the right.

A magnified view of the Zoom cursor

You should repeat this as often as necessary.

Left-click to zoom in, or right-click to zoom out.

The result of zooming in

The Pixel Grid

Paint Shop Pro has a special feature – the Pixel Grid –
which you can invoke when you're viewing images at a
magnification of 10:1 (or greater). Use the Pixel Grid to
make it easier to work with images in detail.

Enabling the Pixel Grid

Pull down the View menu and do the following:

**In version
3, the View
menu is
slightly
different.**

Ensure this is ticked

**Version 4
users can
use the
Style
Palette:**

Click here

**to adjust the
magnification until
it's high enough for
the Grid to display.
(First ensure that
the Zoom icon:**

**is activated in the
Tool Palette).**

Displaying the Pixel Grid

Carry out the appropriate procedures on page 21 to zoom in
on an image. When the magnification is 10:1, the image
looks like this:

A section
of a Paint
Shop Pro
menu . . .

A magnified view of Grid pixels

Full Screen Preview mode

Paint Shop Pro has a special screen mode which shows the current image set against a black background.

Use Full Screen Preview mode to preview changes you've made (and – in version 4 only – as a preliminary to running the more detailed Print Preview mode – see chapter 6).

In version 3, pull down the View menu and click Full Screen.

Entering Full Screen Preview mode

Pull down the View menu and click Full Screen Preview.

An image viewed normally

To return to normal edit mode, press Esc.

The same image in Full Screen Preview mode

Undo and Revert

In version 3, using the Undo command reverses *all* recent actions associated with a specific tool. For instance, if you've applied several fills to an image (without using another tool), Undo rescinds all of them in one go.

In version 4, however, this doesn't happen. Instead, Undo simply revokes the last action. In other words, only the most recent of the several fills is invalidated.

Paint Shop Pro has two features which, effectively, allow you to revert to the way things were *before* you carried out one or more amendments to the active image.

The Undo command

You can 'undo' (i.e. reverse) the last editing action by issuing a menu command.

Pull down the Edit menu and do the following:

Click here

The Revert command

You can – in a single command – undo *all* the editing changes made to an image since it was last saved. You do this by having Paint Shop Pro abandon the changes and reopen the last-saved file.

Pull down the File menu and do the following:

In version 3, the Edit and File menus are slightly different.

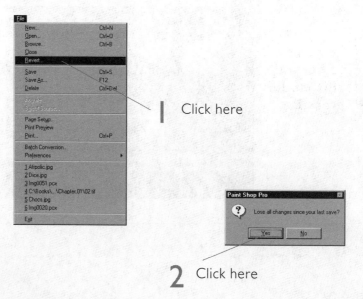

Click here

2 Click here

The Eraser

In version 3, the Eraser is known as the Undo brush. To use it, refer to the Paint Toolbox and do the following:

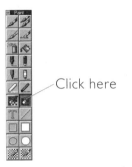

Click here

Now follow the instructions on the right (omitting step 1).

HANDY TIP

Use the Eraser/ Undo brush to carry out *partial* (and highly specific) undos.

There is another technique you can employ to undo editing changes: you can use the Eraser.

The Eraser is actually a Paint Shop Pro tool. (The other tools are covered in later chapters.)

Using the Eraser

Refer to the Tool Palette and do the following:

Click here

The mouse pointer changes (see below). Position the Eraser where you want to begin undoing an effect. Hold down the left-mouse button and drag to undo. Release the mouse button when you've finished.

This image's background has been partially filled with white; here, the Eraser is restoring some of the original black

The original background

Background/foreground colours

Paint Shop Pro uses two broad colour definitions (called 'active' colours):

HANDY TIP

The Colour Palette is normally fixed on the right of the screen. However, as here, it can have an independent existence (and can be dragged, using standard Windows techniques, to any on-screen position). To make the Colour Palette 'float', double-click anywhere in the Select Colour Panel (but outside the colours).

Foreground colours — occupy the foreground of images and are invoked with the left mouse button

Background colours — occupy the background of images and are invoked with the right mouse button

The way you work with foreground and background colours is crucial to your use of Paint Shop Pro. Fortunately, selecting the appropriate colours – via the on-screen Colour Palette – is very easy and straightforward.

The Colour Palette defined

The Colour Palette has the following sections:

REMEMBER

Various methods exist for defining colours numerically. Paint Shop Pro uses the two main ones:

RGB 'Red, Green and Blue'

HSL 'Hue, Saturation and Luminance'

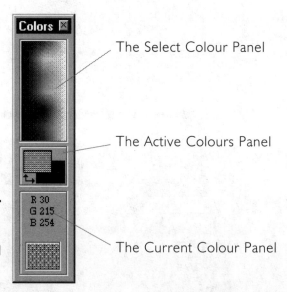

The Select Colour Panel

The Active Colours Panel

The Current Colour Panel

...contd

Using the Select Colour Panel

Move the mouse pointer over the Select Colour Panel. The pointer changes to:

If the active image has 16 million colours, Paint Shop Pro launches the Color dialog after steps 1-2. Omit steps 3 and 4. Instead, select a colour in the Basic Colors section in the Colors dialog, or type in a RGß or HSL definition on the bottom right.
   Finally, click OK.

Position the pointer over the colours in the Select Colour Panel; as you do so, the details in the Current Colour Panel update automatically. When you find the colour you want to use, do ONE of the following:

•   left-click once to select it as a foreground colour

•   right-click once to select it as a background colour

Using the Active Colours Panel

You can use another method to select a foreground/background colour. Refer to the Active Colours Panel. Carry out steps 1, 2 and 4 below to select a foreground colour, OR 2-4 to pick a background colour:

Double-click here: to swap existing foreground and background colours

In version 3, the Active Colours Panel is located in the Select Toolbox.
   In steps 1 and 2, *double*-click to produce the relevant dialog (this is a little different).

| Click here

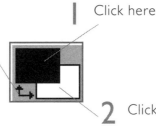

2 Click here

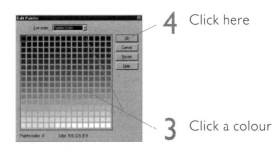

4 Click here

3 Click a colour

The Clear command

You can have Paint Shop Pro automatically replace an image with the current background colour.

This means you can't use standard Windows techniques to paste it back into a Paint Shop Pro window.

Note, however, that Paint Shop Pro does not copy the original image to the Windows Clipboard. If you need to restore the image, however, you can do so by using the Undo feature (see page 26) *providing you perform the undo immediately after the Clear operation.*

Using Clear

Pull down the Edit menu and do the following:

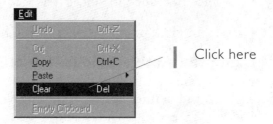

Click here

See the 'before' and 'after' illustrations below:

An image before a Clear operation

The same image after a Clear operation (the background colour was a greyscale)

Making selections

In this chapter, you'll learn about selection types. You'll define rectangular, square, elliptical and circular selections, and several specialist types. You'll also learn to deselect, invert and move selections, then amend feathering/opacity. Finally, you'll save selections for reuse later, and create multiple/subtractive selections.

Chapter Two

Covers

Selections – an overview

Selecting all or part of a Paint Shop Pro image is the essential preliminary for performing any of the many supported editing operations.

You can make the following kinds of selections:

- rectangular

- square

- elliptical

- circular

- freehand

- colour-based

- additive and subtractive

Additionally, you can select an entire image in one operation.

Once part of an image has been selected, you can perform the following, selection-specific operations:

— changing selection modes

— removing (deselecting) selections

— inverting selections

— moving parts of an image

— amending feathering (the degree of hardness with which the selection is drawn)

— adjusting opacity (the degree of transparency)

— specifying a transparent colour (as a means of limiting selections)

You can also save image selections to disk as special files, and then reopen them at will within other images.

REMEMBER

Most of the options on the immediate right are not available in version 3 of Paint Shop Pro.

Selection borders

 You can select all of an image, in one operation (see page 52) but only in version 4.

Generally, whenever you make a selection in Paint Shop Pro, you'll select *part* of an image. Whether you do this or select an image in its entirety, the portion you've selected is surrounded with a dotted line:

A rectangular (regular) selection

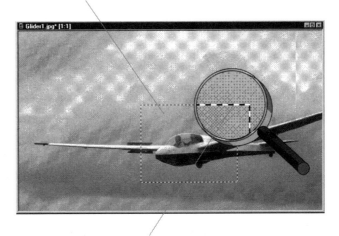

A magnified view of the selection border

Version 3 users utilise the Select Toolbox, instead:

These tools are used

The selection border (sometimes called a 'marquee') moves, which makes it very easy to locate.

In version 4 of Paint Shop Pro, you make partial selections with the help of specific tools within the Tool Palette:

These tools are used

Selection modes

REMEMBER

Version 3 does not support floating selections.

You can use two kinds of selections in Paint Shop Pro:

Standard　These form part of the original image. In other words, if you move a selection area (see pages 50-51), Paint Shop Pro fills the resultant gap with the background colour

Floating　When a selection area is 'floating', the contents are deemed to be on top of (and distinct from) the original

See the illustrations below for a visual demonstration of Standard and Floating selections in action:

A Standard selection. The selection area has been moved, filling the gap with white

A Floating selection. As above, but the underlying image is unaffected

...contd

There is no facility to invert selections in version 3.

Making selections float

First, define a selection area (see pages 36-47 and 58 for how to do this). Now pull down the Selections menu and do the following:

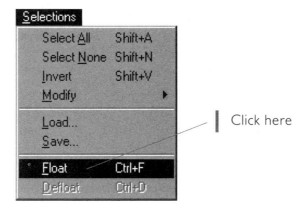

Click here

Paint Shop Pro calls returning a selection area to standard 'defloating' it.

Making selections defloat

After you've defined a selection area (see pages 36-47 and 58) and made it float, pull down the Selections menu and do the following:

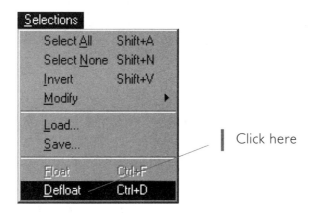

Click here

Selecting rectangles

You can create rectangular selections in two ways:

- with the use of the mouse

- with the use of a special dialog

The mouse route

Ensure the Tool Palette is on-screen (if it isn't, pull down the View menu and click Tool Palette). Then do the following:

Instead of step 1, version 3 users should do the following in the Select Toolbox:

Click here

Omit steps 2 and 3, then proceed to page 37.

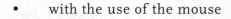

Click here

Now ensure the Style bar is on-screen. Carry out the following steps:

3 Optional – type in a revised feathering

Feathering refers to the sharpness of the selection. Note the following range:

2 Click here; select Rectangle in the list

| 0 | maximum sharpness |
| 20 | maximum softness |

Now carry out the additional procedures on page 37.

...contd

The Rectangle selection cursor looks like this:

Position the mouse pointer where you want the rectangular selection to begin. Hold down the left mouse button and drag to create the selection.

The selection rectangle in the course of being drawn

Instead of step 1, version 3 users should do the following in the Select Toolbox:

Double-click here

Now carry out steps 2 and 3.

Release the button when you've finished.

The dialog route
Refer to the Tool Palette and do the following:

Double-click here

In version 3, the Select Area dialog is slightly different.

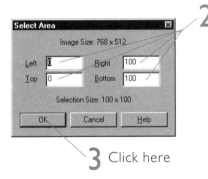

2 Type in the positions of the 4 corners (in pixels)

3 Click here

Selecting squares

Instead of step 1, version 3 users should do the following in the Select Toolbox:

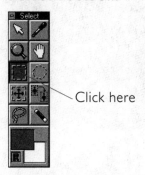

— Click here

Omit steps 2 and 3, then follow the procedures in the HANDY TIP on page 39.

Feathering refers to the sharpness of the selection. Note the following range:

0   maximum sharpness

20   maximum softness

You can create square selections in two ways:

• with the use of the mouse

• with the use of a special dialog

The mouse route

Ensure the Tool Palette is on-screen (if it isn't, pull down the View menu and click Tool Palette). Then do the following:

Click here

Now ensure the Style bar is on-screen. Carry out the following steps:

3 Optional – type in a revised feathering

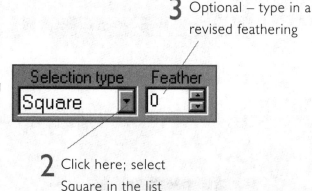

2 Click here; select Square in the list

Now carry out the additional procedures on page 39.

...contd

Position the mouse pointer where you want the square selection to begin. Hold down the left mouse button and drag to create the selection.

There is no separate Square tool in version 3. Instead, hold down Ctrl as you follow these procedures (this forces Paint Shop Pro 3 to define a square).

The square selection in the course of being drawn

Release the button when you've finished.

The dialog route
Refer to the Tool Palette and do the following:

Instead of step 1, version 3 users should do the following in the Select Toolbox:

Double-click here

Double-click here

Now carry out steps 2 and 3.

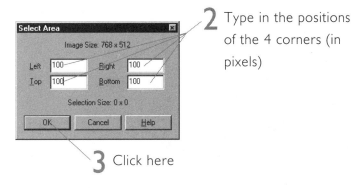

2 Type in the positions of the 4 corners (in pixels)

3 Click here

Selecting ellipses

You can create elliptical selections in the following way:

 Instead of step 1, version 3 users should do the following in the Select Toolbox:

Creating elliptical selections

Ensure the Tool Palette is on-screen (if it isn't, pull down the View menu and click Tool Palette). Then do the following:

| Click here

Click here

Omit steps 2 and 3, then follow the procedures on page 41.

Now ensure the Style bar is on-screen. Carry out the following steps:

3 Optional – type in a revised feathering

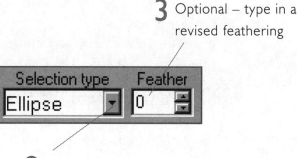

2 Click here; select Ellipse in the list

Now carry out the additional procedures on page 41.

 Feathering refers to the sharpness of the selection. Note the following range:

0   maximum sharpness

20   maximum softness

...contd

The Ellipse selection cursor looks like this:

Position the mouse pointer where you want the elliptical selection to begin. Hold down the left mouse button and drag to create the selection.

The elliptical selection in the course of being drawn

Release the button when you've finished.

This is the result:

A magnified view of part of the final ellipse

Selecting circles

Instead of step 1, version 3 users should do the following in the Select Toolbox:

Click here

Omit steps 2 and 3, then follow the procedures in the HANDY TIP on page 43.

Feathering refers to the sharpness of the selection. Note the following range:

0   maximum sharpness
20   maximum softness

You can define circular selections in the following way:

Creating circular selections

Ensure the Tool Palette is on-screen (if it isn't, pull down the View menu and click Tool Palette). Then do the following:

| Click here

Now ensure the Style bar is on-screen. Carry out the following steps:

3 Optional – type in a revised feathering

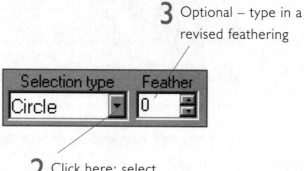

2 Click here; select Circle in the list

Now carry out the additional procedures on page 43.

...contd

Position the mouse pointer where you want the circular selection to begin. Hold down the left mouse button and drag to create the selection.

 There is no separate Circle tool in version 3. Instead, hold down Ctrl as you follow the procedures set out on the right; this forces Paint Shop Pro 3 to define a circle.

The circular selection in the course of being drawn

 The Circle selection cursor looks like this:

Release the button when you've finished.

This is the result:

A magnified view of part of the final circle

Irregular selections

In version 3, the Freehand tool is known as the Lasso.

You can use a special Paint Shop Pro tool – the Freehand tool – to create selections by hand.

Creating freehand selections

Ensure the Tool Palette is on-screen (if it isn't, pull down the View menu and click Tool Palette). Then do the following:

Click here

Instead of step 1, version 3 users should do the following in the Select Toolbox:

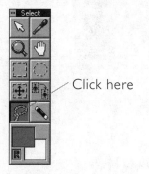

Click here

Omit step 2, then follow the procedures on page 45.

Now ensure the Style bar is on-screen. Carry out the following steps:

2 Optional – type in a revised feathering

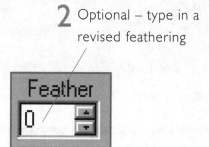

Feathering refers to the sharpness of the selection. Note the following range:

0   maximum sharpness

20   maximum softness

Now carry out the additional procedures on page 45.

...contd

Position the mouse pointer where you want the freehand selection to begin. Hold down the left mouse button and drag to create the selection.

The Freehand (Lasso) cursor looks like this:

The freehand selection in the course of being drawn

Release the button when you've finished.

This is the result:

A magnified view of part of the final freehand selection

Selections based on colour

Instead of steps 1-3, version 3 users should do the following in the Select Toolbox:

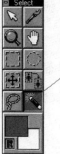

Double-click here

In the Tolerance box in the Magic Wand dialog, insert the correct tolerance. Click OK. Follow the procedures on page 47.

HANDY TIP

Feathering refers to the sharpness of the selection. Note the following range:

0	maximum sharpness
20	maximum softness

You can use another Paint Shop Pro tool – the Magic Wand – to select portions of the active image which share a specific colour.

Creating colour-based selections

Ensure the Tool Palette is on-screen (if it isn't, pull down the View menu and click Tool Palette). Then do the following:

Click here

Now ensure the Style bar is on-screen. Carry out the following steps:

3 Optional – type in a revised tolerance

4 Optional – type in a revised feathering

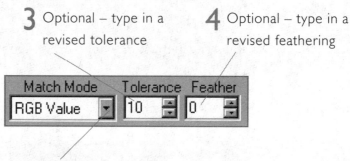

2 Click here; select a selection method

(See the HANDY TIP on page 47 for a definition of tolerance).

Now carry out the additional procedures on page 47.

...contd

Position the mouse pointer over the area you want to select:

HANDY TIP

Re. step 3 overleaf – tolerance refers to the degree to which pixels in an image must approach the chosen pixel for selection to take place. Note the following range:

0   no latitude; only exact matches result in selection

20   maximum tolerance; all pixels are selected

A magnified view of the Magic Wand

Left-click once. This is the result:

A magnified view of part of the colour selection

Deselecting selections

You can disable selections you've already made in two ways:

The menu route

Pull down the Selections menu and do the following:

The menu route is not available to version 3 users.

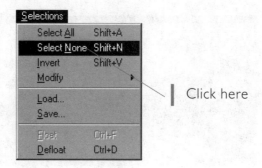

Click here

For version 3 users, the applicable tools are (in the Select Toolbox):

Follow step 1 on the right.

The mouse route

Provided either of these tools are active in the Tool Palette:

You can do the following:

Right-click once

Inverting selections

There is no facility to invert selections in version 3.

When you've selected a portion of an image, you can have Paint Shop Pro do BOTH of the following:

- deselect the selected area

- select the area which was previously unselected

Paint Shop Pro calls this 'inverting a selection'. Use inversion as a means of creating selections which would otherwise be difficult – or impossible – to achieve.

When you invert freehand selections, Paint Shop Pro may not display the inversion accurately. However, any editing changes you make to the selected area will display correctly.

Inverting a selection

First make a normal selection. Then pull down the Selections menu and click Invert.

The illustrations below show inversion in action:

A standard rectangular selection

Paint Shop Pro has also surrounded the selected area (here, the image minus the rectangle) with a dotted border.

The dotted border now denotes the *unselected* area . . .

Moving selections

Version 4 users should ensure the selection frame has not been made floating (see pages 34-35) before carrying out step 1.

Instead of step 1, version 3 users should do the following in the Select Toolbox:

Click here

Move the mouse pointer over the selection area. Hold down the *left* mouse button; drag the area to the new location. Release the button.

Paint Shop Pro lets you move selection areas. You can do this in two ways:

• you can move just the frame which defines the selection area

OR

• you can move the frame AND the contents

Moving selection frames only

Refer to the Tool Palette and do the following:

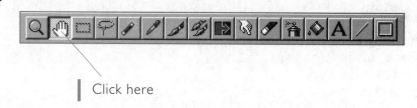

Click here

Now place the mouse pointer over the selection area; it changes to:

Hold down the *right* mouse button; drag the selection. Release the mouse button.

A selection frame being moved

...contd

This technique for moving selection frames and contents is not available in version 3.

Instead, use standard Windows copy-and-paste or cut-and-paste techniques.

Moving selection frames and contents

First, ensure that the selection area is standard or Floating, according to the effect you want to achieve. (See page 35 for a description of the two possible effects). Then refer to the Tool Palette and do the following:

Click one of these

Place the mouse pointer over the selection area; the pointer changes to a four-headed arrow:

Magnified view of Move cursor

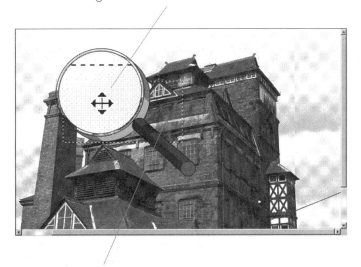

Selection area

Hold down the left mouse button and drag the area to a new location. Release the button to confirm the move.

Selecting an entire image

If you want to work with the whole of an image, you can use a shortcut to select it in its entirety.

Selecting all of the active image

Pull down the Selections menu and do the following:

Version 3 does not allow you to select the whole of an image in one operation.

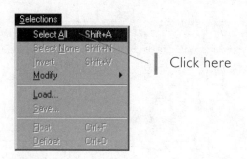

Click here

The illustration below shows an image which has been completely selected:

A magnified view of part of the selection border which surrounds the entire image

Amending selection feathering

As we've seen, when you define a selection within an image, you have the opportunity to customise the feathering. However, you can also do this (and to a greater extent) *after* the selection area has been created.

There is no facility to amend selection feathering in version 3.

Imposing a new feathering

Define a selection. Pull down the Selections menu and click Modify, Feather. Now do the following:

Type in a new feathering

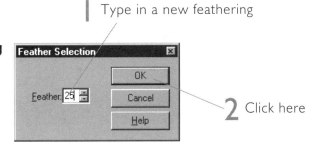

2 Click here

Feathering refers to the sharpness of the selection. Note the following range:

0   maximum sharpness
40   maximum softness

The change in feathering barely displays on screen. However, the illustration below (where a circular selection has been made, the feathering has been changed and the selection has been dragged to one side) shows the change to much greater effect:

Magnified view of feathered selection edge

The selection has been dragged to the left

Amending selection opacity

Another selection feature you can customise is opacity (the degree – or otherwise – of transparency). You can only do this after the selection area has been defined

Imposing a new opacity

Define a selection. Pull down the Selections menu and click Modify, Overall Opacity. Now do the following:

Type in a new opacity

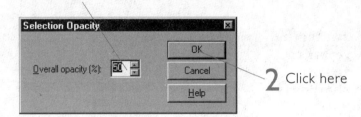

2 Click here

Note the following opacity range:

1	maximum transparency
100	normal opacity
200	maximum opacity

In the illustration below, a rectangular selection has been made. The opacity has then been amended to 50, and the selection has been dragged to one side.

The area of the original selection is semi-opaque

The moved selection is also semi-opaque; the underlying image section is partially visible

Selecting a transparent colour

You can specify a transparent colour; this tells Paint Shop Pro to deselect it within a selection.

REMEMBER **There is no facility to deselect colours in** version 3.

Selecting a colour

Define a selection. Pull down the Selections menu and click Modify, Transparent Color. Now do the following:

Click here; select a colour in the list

HANDY TIP **Note the following opacity range:**

1	maximum transparency
100	normal opacity
200	maximum opacity

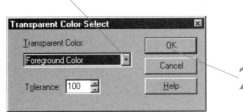

2 Click here

In the illustration below, a rectangular selection was made. A transparent colour (one of the colours in the chimney) was selected, and the selection was dragged to one side.

HANDY TIP **Re. step 1 – the Transparent Color Select dialog only lets you select a few basic colours.**
 For more precision, follow the procedures on page 29 to select a specific background or foreground colour, then select Foreground Color or Background Color.
 Finally, follow step 2.

Only part of the selection has been moved

Part of the selection (corresponding to the selected colour) has been left behind

Reusing selections

Paint Shop Pro lets you save a selection area (the frame, NOT the contents) to disk, as a special file. You can then load it into a new image. This is a convenient way to reuse complex selections.

An unusual selection, saved to disk . . .

REMEMBER

Version 3 does not allow selections to be saved to disk.

HANDY TIP

See page 58 for how to create multiple selections like this.

. . . and then loaded into another image

...contd

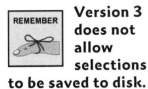

Version 3 does not allow selections to be saved to disk.

Saving a selection

Define a selection. Pull down the Selections menu and click Save. Now do the following:

| Click here. In the drop-down list, click a drive/folder combination

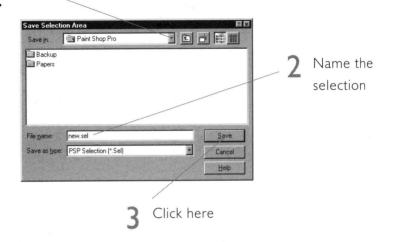

2 Name the selection

3 Click here

Loading a selection

Pull down the Selections menu and click Load. Now do the following:

Re. step 2 – selection files have the following suffix: .SEL

| Click here. In the drop-down list, click a drive/folder combination

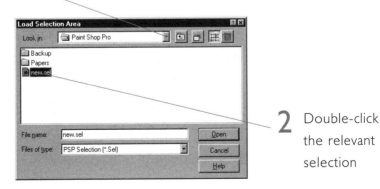

2 Double-click the relevant selection

Selection additions/subtractions

You can define *multiple* selections. This is a very useful technique which enables you to create spectacular effects.

Version 3 does not allow the creation of multiple selections, or selection subtractions.

In the illustration below, a rectangular selection was defined. Then a circle was defined and added to the original selection:

Two joint selections

Creating multiple selections

Define one selection area. Hold down one Shift key as you define another (the two selection areas do not have to be contiguous or overlap). Release the mouse button when you've finished. Repeat as often as necessary.

Subtracting from selections

Define one or more selection areas. Hold down one Ctrl key as you define another which encroaches onto an existing area. Release the mouse button when you've finished. Repeat as often as necessary.

Here, a new circle has been defined, removing part of the original selection

Painting/drawing

Chapter Three

In this chapter, you'll learn how to create a variety of painting/drawing effects. You'll perform freehand painting; copy colours; carry out colour substitutions; select specific colours for foreground/background use; retouch images; carry out spray painting; and fill images with colours, other images and gradients. Finally, you'll format and insert text, and create lines and shapes.

Covers

Painting and drawing – an overview

 Version 3 of Paint Shop Pro uses the Paint Toolbox instead:

Paint Shop Pro lets you paint and draw on-screen, using a variety of specialist tools located within the Tools Palette:

 Version 3's painting/ drawing tools

All the tools within these lines relate to painting and drawing

You can:

*   create freehand paintings/drawings

*   copy colours within images

*   carry out colour substitutions

*   select existing colours as active foreground or background colours

 See the relevant topics later for restrictions which apply to version 3.

*   carry out image retouching

*   carry out spray painting/drawing

*   fill images with colours

*   fill images with patterns

*   fill images with gradients

*   format and insert text into images

*   create lines

*   create shapes

The Paintbrush tool – an overview

Using the Paintbrush tool, you can create

- painting effects
- automated lines

Whichever function you use, you can specify the following components:

In version 3, you can only specify the following settings:

Brush style — Equates to brush shape

Brush size — The range is 1:32

The brush type	You can choose from: Normal, Pen, Pencil, Marker, Crayon, Chalk, Charcoal
The brush size	The permissible range is: 1:200
The brush shape	You can choose from: Square, Round, Left Slash, Right Slash, Horizontal, Vertical
The paper texture	Determines the type of background the painting/ drawing has. You can choose from 29 special effects. These include: Marble, Ocean, Lava, Fog, Canvas, Polka Dot

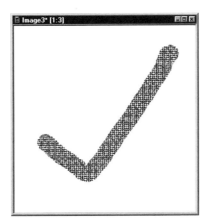

A shape drawn with the following settings:

Brush type = Marker

Size = 90

Shape = Round

Paper texture = Polka Dot

Painting with the Paintbrush tool

REMEMBER

Instead of step 1, version 3 users should do the following in the Paint Toolbox:

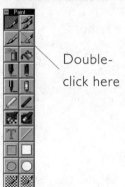

Double-click here

Omit steps 2-5. Complete this dialog:

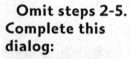
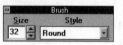

Now follow the procedures in the REMEMBER tip on page 63.

HANDY TIP

Re. step 3 – the available brush size range is:

1	very small
200	very large

Do the following to create painting effects in Paint Shop Pro:

Creating a painting

Ensure the Tool Palette is on-screen (if it isn't, pull down the View menu and click Tool Palette). Then do the following:

Click here

Now ensure the Style bar is on-screen. Carry out the following steps:

3 Type in a brush size

5 Click here; select a texture in the list

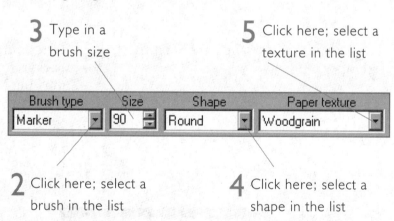

2 Click here; select a brush in the list

4 Click here; select a shape in the list

Now carry out the additional procedures on page 63.

...contd

If you want to limit the painting to a selected area, make a selection first.

Now follow the procedures on pages 28-29 to select the appropriate foreground or background colour. Position the mouse pointer where you want the painting to begin. Do one of the following:

A.   To paint with the current foreground colour, hold down the *left* mouse button and drag

B.   To paint with the current background colour, hold down the *right* mouse button and drag

Version 3 users should do the following in the Paint Toolbox:

Click here

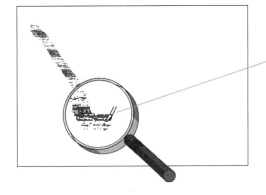

A magnified view of the Paintbrush pointer

Release the button when you've finished.

Now carry out the relevant procedures on the right.

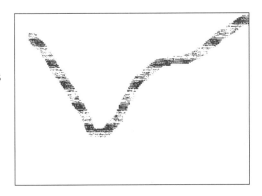

The completed painting

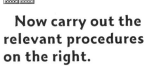

Drawing with the Paintbrush tool

Do the following to automate the creation of lines in Paint Shop Pro:

 REMEMBER **Version 3 users can't draw lines with this technique. However, see pages 92-93.**

 HANDY TIP **Version 4 users can also use the Line tool to draw lines – see pages 92-93.**

Drawing lines

Ensure the Tool Palette is on-screen (if it isn't, pull down the View menu and click Tool Palette). Then do the following:

Click here

Now ensure the Style bar is on-screen. Carry out the following steps:

HANDY TIP **Re. step 3 – the available brush size range is:**

1	very small
200	very large

3 Type in a brush size

5 Click here; select a texture in the list

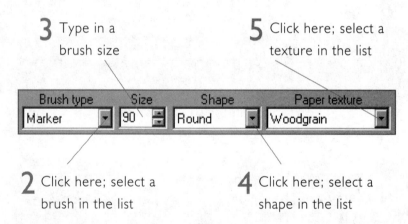

2 Click here; select a brush in the list

4 Click here; select a shape in the list

Now carry out the additional procedures on page 65.

...contd

If you want to limit line creation to a selected area, make a selection first.

Now follow the procedures on pages 28-29 to select the appropriate foreground or background colour. Position the mouse pointer where you want the line to begin. Do one of the following:

A. To draw with the current foreground colour, hold down the *left* mouse button and click once

B. To draw with the current background colour, hold down the *right* mouse button and click once

Now hold down one Shift key and left- or right-click where you want the first segment of the line to end.

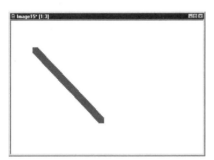

The first line

segment

To create another segment, continue to hold down the Shift key and left- or right-click elsewhere:

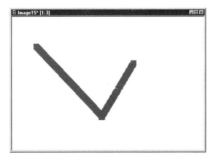

Two line

segments

Repeat this process as often as necessary.

Copying with the Clone brush

Instead of step 1, version 3 users should do the following in the Paint Toolbox:

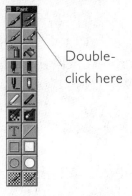

Double-click here

Omit steps 2-6. Complete this dialog:

Now follow the procedures in the REMEMBER tip on page 67.

Cloning is the copying of colour from one location within an image to another (or to another image which has the same number of colours). To clone colours, you use the Clone brush.

Cloning

Ensure the Tool Palette is on-screen (if it isn't, pull down the View menu and click Tool Palette). Then do the following:

Click here

Now ensure the Style bar is on-screen. Carry out the following steps:

3 Type in a brush size

4 Type in an opacity

6 Click here; select a texture in the list

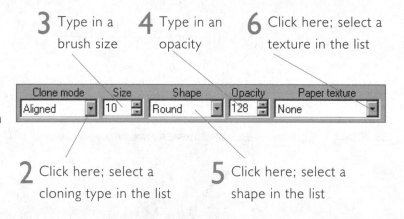

2 Click here; select a cloning type in the list

5 Click here; select a shape in the list

Now carry out the additional procedures on page 67.

Re. step 4 – the available opacity range is:

I	very nearly transparent
128	entirely opaque

...contd

Version 3 users should do the following in the Paint Toolbox:

Click here

Now carry out the procedures on the right.

The Clone crosshairs indicate the pixel which is to be copied.

Position the mouse pointer over the image section you want to copy:

A magnified view of the Clone cursor

Right-click once (your PC will beep). Perform step 1 below:

The Clone crosshairs

Position the cursor where you want to insert the colour marked by the crosshairs

Finally, hold down the left mouse button and drag (repeatedly) to perform the copy. Release the button when you've finished.

Replacing colours globally

Instead of step 1, version 3 users should do the following in the Paint Toolbox:

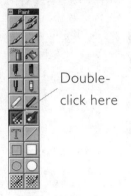

Double-click here

You can have Paint Shop Pro replace a specified colour with another. You do this by nominating the colour you want to replace as the foreground colour, then selecting the new colour as the background colour. (Or vice versa).

You can replace colours:

- globally (within the whole of an image, or a selection area)

- manually (by using the Color Replacer tool as a brush)

Carrying out a global substitution

Ensure the Tool Palette is on-screen (if it isn't, pull down the View menu and click Tool Palette). Then do the following:

Omit steps 2-5. Complete this dialog:

Now follow the procedures in the REMEMBER tip on page 69.

Click here

Now ensure the Style bar is on-screen. Carry out the following steps:

3 Type in a brush size

5 Click here; select a texture in the list

Re. step 4 – the available tolerance range is:

0   only exact matches are replaced

200 every pixel is replaced

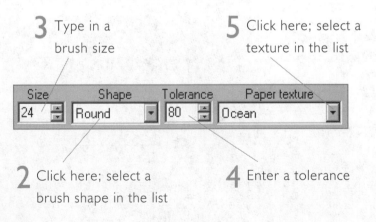

2 Click here; select a brush shape in the list

4 Enter a tolerance

Now carry out the additional procedures on page 69.

...contd

 If you want to limit the exchange to a selected area, make a selection first. Then carry out A. or B. *within the selection.*

Now follow the procedures on pages 28-29 to select the appropriate foreground and/or background colour. Do one of the following:

A.   To replace the background with the foreground colour, double-click anywhere in the image with the *left* mouse button

B.   To replace the foreground with the background colour, double-click anywhere in the image with the *right* mouse button

The illustrations below demonstrate the result of performing a colour replace operation:

 Version 3 users should do the following in the Paint Toolbox:

 Click here

Now carry out step A. or B. on the right.

The original image

The green of the grass has been replaced with white

Replacing colours manually

Instead of step 1, version 3 users should do the following in the Paint Toolbox:

Double-click here

Omit steps 2-5. Complete this dialog:

Now follow the procedures in the REMEMBER tip on page 71.

Re. step 4 – the available tolerance range is:

0 only exact matches are replaced

200 every pixel is replaced

To replace colours manually (i.e. by using the Color Replacer tool as a brush), carry out the following procedures.

Replacing colours manually requires a light touch (and experimentation with the available settings – see steps 2-5 below).

Carrying out a manual substitution

Ensure the Tool Palette is on-screen (if it isn't, pull down the View menu and click Tool Palette). Then do the following:

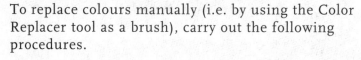

Click here

Now ensure the Style bar is on-screen. Carry out the following steps:

3 Type in a brush size

5 Click here; select a texture in the list

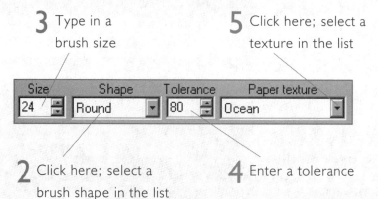

2 Click here; select a brush shape in the list

4 Enter a tolerance

Now carry out the additional procedures on page 71.

...contd

If you want to limit the exchange to a selected area, make a selection first. Then carry out step A. or B. within the selection.

Now follow the procedures on pages 28-29 to select the appropriate foreground and/or background colour. Position the mouse pointer where you want the manual colour substitution to take place. Do one of the following:

A.   To replace the background with the foreground colour, hold down the *left* mouse button

B.   To replace the foreground with the background colour, hold down the *right* mouse button

Now do the following:

Version 3 users should do the following in the Paint Toolbox:

 Click here

Now carry out step A. or B. on the right. Finally, perform step 1.

Drag over the appropriate area to carry out the substitution

A magnified view of the Color Replace cursor in action

Release the mouse button when you've finished.

Replacing colours with lines

The Color Replacer tool also lets you substitute colours as you create lines.

Version 3 users can't draw lines with this technique. However, see pages 92-93.

Replacing colours with lines requires a light touch (and experimentation with the available settings – see steps 2-5 below).

Replacing colours while drawing lines

Ensure the Tool Palette is on-screen (if it isn't, pull down the View menu and click Tool Palette). Then do the following:

Version 4 users can also use the Line tool to draw lines – see pages 92-93.

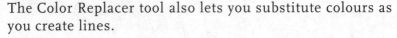

| Click here

Now ensure the Style bar is on-screen. Carry out the following steps:

Re. step 3 – the available brush size range is:

| 1 | very small |
| 200 | very large |

3 Type in a brush size

5 Click here; select a texture in the list

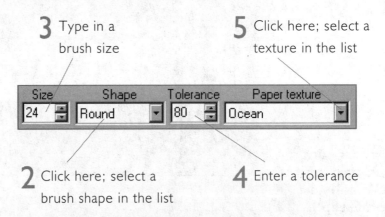

2 Click here; select a brush shape in the list

4 Enter a tolerance

Now carry out the additional procedures on page 73.

...contd

If you want to limit the exchange to a selected area, make a selection first.

Now follow the procedures on pages 28-29 to select the appropriate foreground or background colour. Position the mouse pointer where you want the colour replacement to begin. Do one of the following:

A.   To draw with the current foreground colour, hold down the *left* mouse button and click once

B.   To draw with the current background colour, hold down the *right* mouse button and click once

Now hold down one Shift key and left- or right-click where you want the first segment of the line to end.

The first line segment

Here, the green of the grass is being replaced with white.

To create another segment, continue to hold down the Shift key and left- or right-click elsewhere:

The second line segment

Repeat this process as often as necessary.

Using the Dropper tool

In version 4, you can activate the Dropper (within most paint tools) by holding down one Ctrl key.

The Dropper (the Eyedropper, in version 3) is an extremely useful tool which you can use to:

1. select a colour in the active image

2. nominate this as the active foreground or background colour

Because the Dropper is so useful when you're painting and drawing, you can also use a special shortcut to access it directly, without selecting the Dropper icon in the Tool Palette.

Instead of step 1, version 3 users should do the following in the Select Toolbox:

Using the Dropper
Ensure the Tool Palette is on-screen (if it isn't, pull down the View menu and click Tool Palette). Then do the following:

Click here

Click here

Now position the mouse pointer over the colour you want to pick up. Left-click once to nominate it as the foreground colour, or right-click once to nominate it as the background colour.

Now carry out the procedures on the right.

Here, left-clicking has inserted this colour:
in the Colour Palette.

The selected colour has appeared here

Retouching – an overview

You can use the Retouch tool to perform the following photoretouching operations on images (or selection areas within images):

The only retouching options available in version 3 are:
- Smoothing
- Sharpening

Lightening	makes the image or selection brighter
Darkening	makes the image or selection darker
Softening	mutes the image or selection and diminishes contrast
Sharpening	emphasises edges and accentuates contrast
Embossing	produces a raised ('stamped') effect (where the foreground is emphasised in relation to the background)
Smudging	produces a stained, blurred effect

You can't perform retouching operations *globally.*

However, there are three exceptions to this:
— Embossing
— Softening
— Sharpening

In both version 3 and 4 of Paint Shop Pro, you can apply a special filter to achieve these effects:
- on the whole of an image
- on a specific selection area

See Chapter 4 for more information.

You can use the Retouch tool in the following ways:

— as a brush

— to draw lines

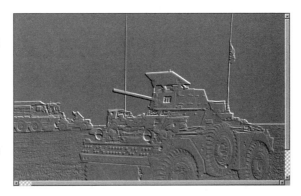

An entire image, embossed

Retouching images manually

Version 3 users can only perform Smooth or Sharpen operations.

Instead of step 1, do the following in the Paint Toolbox:

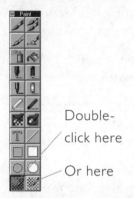

Double-click here

Or here

Omit steps 2-6. Complete the dialog which launches. Now follow the procedures in the REMEMBER tip on page 77.

To retouch images manually (i.e. by using the Retouch tool as a brush), carry out the procedures described below.

Retouching images manually requires a light touch (and experimentation with the available settings – see steps 2-6 below).

Carrying out a manual retouch operation

Ensure the Tool Palette is on-screen (if it isn't, pull down the View menu and click Tool Palette). Then do the following:

| Click here

Now ensure the Style bar is on-screen. Carry out the following steps:

2 Click here; select a retouch tool

6 Click here; select a texture in the list

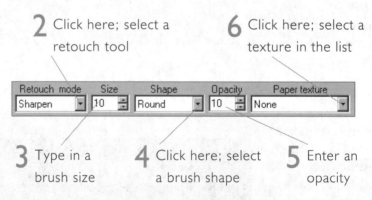

3 Type in a brush size

4 Click here; select a brush shape

5 Enter an opacity

Now carry out the additional procedures on page 77.

Re. step 4 – the available opacity range is:

1   very nearly transparent

128   entirely opaque

...contd

 If you want to limit the retouching operation to a selected area, make a selection first. Then carry out step 1 *within the selection*.

Position the mouse pointer where you want the retouching operation specified in step 2 on page 76 to take place. The pointer looks like this:

In version 3, however, the Smooth and Sharpen pointers are as follows:

 Sharpen tool

 Smooth tool

Hold down the left mouse button and do the following:

 To perform a Smooth or Sharpen operation, Version 3 users should do one of the following in the Paint Toolbox:

Click here to Sharpen

Click here to Smooth

Now carry out step 1 on the right.

Drag over the appropriate area to carry out the retouching operation

A magnified view of the results of applying a Smudging operation

Retouching images with lines

To retouch images by defining lines, carry out the procedures described below.

Retouching images while drawing lines

Ensure the Tool Palette is on-screen (if it isn't, pull down the View menu and click Tool Palette). Then do the following:

Version 3 users cannot perform Smooth and Sharpen operations in this way.

| Click here

Now ensure the Style bar is on-screen. Carry out the following steps:

2 Click here; select a retouch tool

6 Click here; select a texture in the list

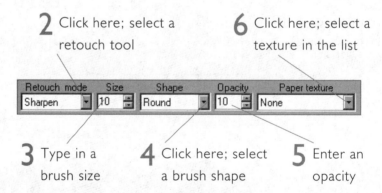

3 Type in a brush size

4 Click here; select a brush shape

5 Enter an opacity

Re. step 4 – the available opacity range is:

1   very nearly transparent

128 entirely opaque

Now carry out the additional procedures on page 79.

...contd

Position the mouse pointer where you want the retouching operation specified in step 2 on page 78 to take place. The pointer looks like this:

Position the mouse pointer where you want the retouching operation specified in step 2 on page 78 to take place.

If you want to limit the retouching operation to a selected area, make a selection first. Then carry out the procedures on the right *within the selection*.

Left-click where you want the linear retouching operation to begin. Now hold down one Shift key and left-click where you want the first segment of the line to end.

The first line segment, drawn with the Embossed tool

To create another segment, continue to hold down the Shift key and left- or right-click elsewhere:

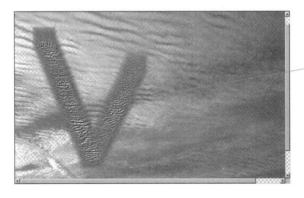

The second line segment

Repeat this process as often as necessary.

Painting with the Airbrush

Instead of step 1, version 3 users should do the following in the Paint Toolbox:

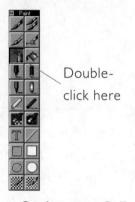

Double-click here

Omit steps 2-5. Complete the dialog which launches. Now follow the procedures in the REMEMBER tip on page 81.

You can use the Airbrush tool to simulate painting with a spray can. You can do this in two ways:

- while using the Airbrush as a brush

- while using the Airbrush to draw lines

Using the Airbrush as a brush

Ensure the Tool Palette is on-screen (if it isn't, pull down the View menu and click Tool Palette). Then do the following:

Click here

Now ensure the Style bar is on-screen. Carry out the following steps:

3 Type in a brush size

5 Click here; select a texture in the list

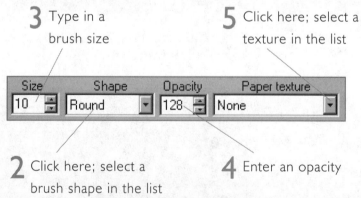

Re. step 4 – the available opacity range is:

| 1 | very nearly transparent |
| 128 | entirely opaque |

2 Click here; select a brush shape in the list

4 Enter an opacity

Now carry out the additional procedures on page 81.

...contd

If you want to limit the airbrush operation to a selected area, make a selection first. Then carry out step 1 *within the selection.*

Now follow the procedures on pages 28-29 to select the appropriate foreground and/or background colour. Position the mouse pointer where you want the airbrush operation to take place. Do one of the following:

A. To paint with the foreground colour, hold down the *left* mouse button

B. To paint with the background colour, hold down the *right* mouse button

Now do the following:

Version 3 users should do the following in the Paint Toolbox:

Drag over the appropriate area

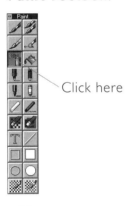

Click here

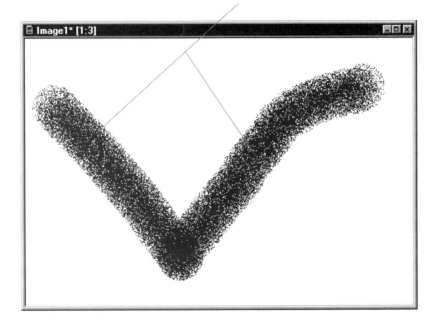

Now carry out step 1 on the right.

The Airbrush cursor looks like this:

Release the mouse button when you've finished.

Drawing with the Airbrush

To define lines with the Airbrush tool, carry out the following procedures.

Using the Airbrush to draw lines

Ensure the Tool Palette is on-screen (if it isn't, pull down the View menu and click Tool Palette). Then do the following:

| Click here

Now ensure the Style bar is on-screen. Carry out the following steps:

3 Type in a brush size

5 Click here; select a texture in the list

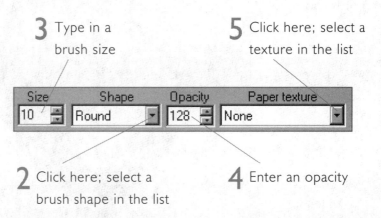

2 Click here; select a brush shape in the list

4 Enter an opacity

Now carry out the additional procedures on page 83.

...contd

Now follow the procedures on pages 28-29 to select the appropriate foreground or background colour. Position the mouse pointer where you want the airbrush operation to take place. Do one of the following:

pages 28-29

If you want to limit the airbrush operation to a selected area, make a selection first. Then carry out the procedures on the right *within the selection*.

A.   To paint with the foreground colour, hold down the *left* mouse button

B.   To paint with the background colour, hold down the *right* mouse button

Left- or right-click where you want the line to begin. Hold down one Shift key and click where you want the first segment of the line to end.

The Airbrush cursor looks like this:

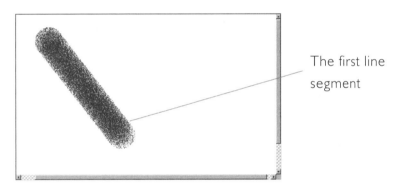

The first line segment

To create another segment, continue to hold down the Shift key and left- or right-click elsewhere:

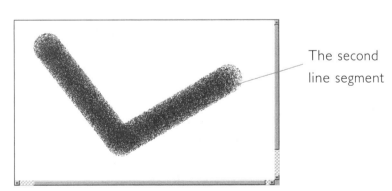

The second line segment

Repeat this process as often as necessary.

Inserting colours with the Fill tool

Instead of step 1, version 3 users should do the following in the Paint Toolbox:

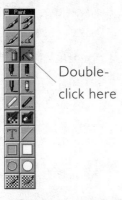

Double-click here

Omit steps 2-4. Complete the dialog which launches. Now follow the procedures in the REMEMBER tip on page 85.

Re. step 3 – the available tolerance range is:

0   only exact matches are filled

200   every pixel is filled

You can use the Fill tool to

- fill an image with colour

- fill an image with a specific pattern (Paint Shop Pro defines 'patterns' as images you've already opened into additional windows)

- fill an image with a gradient (Paint Shop Pro supports 4 kinds: Linear, Rectangular, Sunburst, Radial)

Filling images with a colour

Ensure the Tool Palette is on-screen (if it isn't, pull down the View menu and click Tool Palette). Then do the following:

Click here

Now ensure the Style bar is on-screen. Carry out the following steps:

2 Click here; choose a selection method

4 Click here; select Solid Color

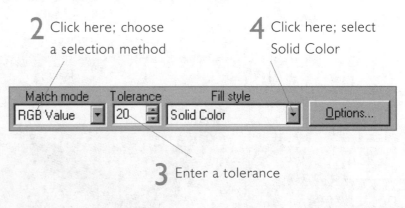

3 Enter a tolerance

Now carry out the additional procedures on page 85.

...contd

HANDY TIP

If you want to limit the fill operation to a selected area, make a selection first. Then carry out step 1 or 2 *within the selection*.

Now follow the procedures on pages 28-29 to select the appropriate foreground and/or background colour. Position the mouse pointer where you want the fill operation to take place. The cursor changes to:

Now perform step 1 below to insert the foreground colour, OR step 2 to insert the background colour:

REMEMBER

Version 3 users should do the following in the Paint Toolbox:

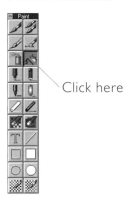

Click here

Now carry out step 1 OR 2 on the right.

Left-click once

2 Right-click once

In the above illustration, part of the car has been filled with a light greyscale.

Inserting patterns with the Fill tool

If you want, you can also select part of the image in the normal way.

  If you do this, carrying out step 1 on page 87 ensures that Paint Shop Pro 4 only inserts the selected portion of the image as a pattern.

Filling images with a pattern

First, open the image you want to insert as a pattern. Ensure the Tool Palette is on-screen (if it isn't, pull down the View menu and click Tool Palette). Then do the following:

| Click here

Now ensure the Style bar is on-screen. Carry out the following steps:

2 Click here; choose a selection method

4 Click here; select Pattern

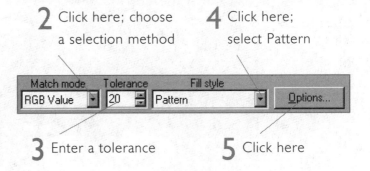

Version 3 users cannot insert pattern fills.

3 Enter a tolerance

5 Click here

Re. step 3 – the available tolerance range is:

0   only exact matches are filled

200   every pixel is filled

6 Click here; select a pattern

7 Click here

Now carry out the additional procedures on page 87.

...contd

Now click the window which hosts the image into which you want to insert the pattern. Position the mouse pointer where you want to insert it (inside a selection area, if you defined one – see the HANDY TIP on page 86).

The cursor changes to:

If you want to limit the pattern insertion operation to a selected area (as in the illustration on the right), make a selection first. Then carry out step 1 *within the selection.*

For help with creating patterns for use with the Fill tool, version 4 users should refer to pages 160-161.

Perform step 1 below:

Left- or right-click once

This area was
pre-selected

In the above illustration (see the magnified portion), part of the car has been filled with a section from another image.

Inserting gradients with the Fill tool

Version 3 users cannot insert gradient fills.

Filling images with a gradient

Ensure the Tool Palette is on-screen (if it isn't, pull down the View menu and click Tool Palette). Then do the following:

| Click here

Re. steps 6 and 7 – Paint Shop Pro 4 supports two basic gradient types: linear and non-linear (Rectangular, Sunburst and Radial).
   In linear gradients, you specify the angle; in non-linear, you specify the point of origin.

Now ensure the Style bar is on-screen. Carry out the following steps:

2 Click here; choose a selection method

4 Click here; select a gradient type

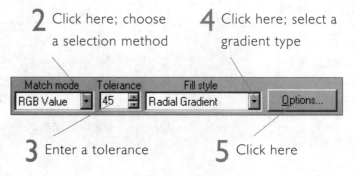

3 Enter a tolerance

5 Click here

Re. steps 6 and 7 – if you're defining a *linear* gradient, the dialog which launches is different.
   In the Drag field, insert the gradient angle. Click OK.

6 Enter gradient coordinates (as a % of height/width)

7 Click here

Now carry out the additional procedures on page 89.

...contd

If you want to limit the gradient operation to a selected area, make a selection first. Then carry out the procedure on the right *within the selection*.

Position the mouse pointer where you want to insert the gradient fill. The cursor changes to:

Now left- or right-click once (but see the REMEMBER tip).

Note that left-clicking defines a gradient from the foreground to the background colour, while right-clicking defines from the background to the foreground colour.

A Radial gradient

A Sunburst gradient

A Rectangular gradient

Inserting text with the Text tool

Paint Shop Pro lets you insert text into images, easily and conveniently. In the process, you can apply:

1.   a typeface and/or type size

2.   a style. With most typefaces, you can choose from:

     — Regular

     — *Italic*

     — **Bold**

     — ***Bold/Italic***

3.   the following text effects

     — ~~Strikeout~~

     — <u>Underline</u>

4.   an alignment. You can choose from:

     — Left

     — Center

     — Right

You can also specify whether the text you insert is 'Standard' or 'Floating'. (See page 34). Additionally, you can elect to have Paint Shop Pro 'anti-alias' the text.

Text inserted into an image

...contd

Instead of step 1, version 3 users should do the following in the Paint Toolbox:

Click here

Now complete the Add Text dialog. Click OK.

Version 4 users should click Floating to have the inserted text 'float'.

Inserting text

If you want the text you create to be inserted in the current foreground colour, follow the procedures on page 28 to select the appropriate colour (and carry out the procedure in the HANDY TIP below). Ensure the Tool Palette is on-screen (if it isn't, pull down the View menu and click Tool Palette). Then do the following:

Click here

Now position the mouse pointer where you want the text inserted. Left-click once. Carry out the following steps:

2 Click a font   3 Click a style   4 Enter a typesize

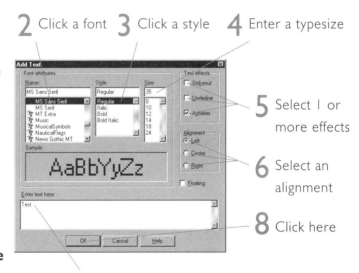

5 Select 1 or more effects

6 Select an alignment

8 Click here

7 Enter the relevant text here

Drawing with the Line tool

 Instead of step 1, version 3 users should do the following in the Paint Toolbox:

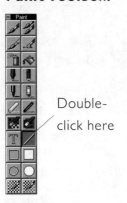

Double-click here

Omit step 2. In the Width field in the Line dialog, type in a line width. Now follow the procedures in the REMEMBER tip on page 93.

 In version 4, the Line tool cursor looks like this:

On pages 64-65, we looked at a shortcut to line creation. However, Paint Shop Pro has a separate tool which you can use to create more detailed lines.

You can:

- define freehand lines

- have Paint Shop Pro restrict the line you create to 45° increments

Drawing lines

Ensure the Tool Palette is on-screen (if it isn't, pull down the View menu and click Tool Palette). Then do the following:

Click here

Now ensure the Style bar is on-screen. Carry out the following step:

2 Type in a line width

Now carry out the additional procedures on page 93.

...contd

To constrain the line to 45° increments, version 4 users should hold down one Shift key during the drag operation.

Now follow the procedures on pages 28-29 to select the appropriate foreground or background colour. Position the mouse pointer where you want the line to begin. Do one of the following:

A. To draw with the current foreground colour, hold down the *left* mouse button

B. To draw with the current background colour, hold down the *right* mouse button

Now drag out the first line segment.

In version 3, the Line tool cursor looks like this:

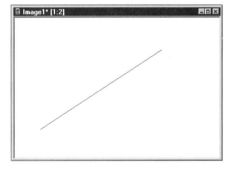

The first line segment
– Paint Shop Pro
inserts a marker line
(in version 4 only)

Now release the mouse button. Paint Shop Pro inserts the full line:

Version 3 users should do the following in the Paint Toolbox:

Click here

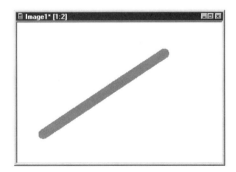

The completed
line segment

Now carry out the procedures on the right.

Drawing with the Shape tool

REMEMBER

Instead of step 1, version 3 users should do the following in the Paint Toolbox:

You can use the Shape tool to create rectangles, squares, circles and ellipses.

Using the Shape tool

Ensure the Tool Palette is on-screen (if it isn't, pull down the View menu and click Tool Palette). Then do the following:

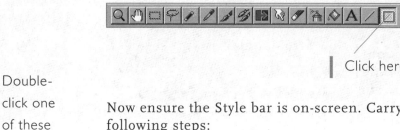

Click here

Double-click one of these

Or one of these

Now ensure the Style bar is on-screen. Carry out the following steps:

2 Click here; choose a shape

If appropriate, complete the dialog which launches.
To draw the required shape, click the relevant tool icon (as above). Then follow step A. OR B. on the right.

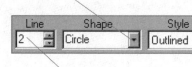

3 Enter a line width

4 Click here; select a style

First, follow the procedures on pages 28-29 to select the appropriate foreground or background colour. Position the mouse pointer where you want the shape to begin. Now do one of the following:

HANDY TIP

Re. step 4 – version 4 users can create filled shapes (choose Filled), or merely outlines (choose Outlined).

A. To draw with the current foreground colour, hold down the *left* mouse button

B. To draw with the current background colour, hold down the *right* mouse button

Now drag out the shape. Release the mouse button when you've finished.

Using filters

In this chapter, you'll learn how to add a variety of creative effects to images (or image selections). You'll do this by applying any of Paint Shop Pro's numerous filters. Finally, you'll create your own filters; amend user-defined filters; and apply these to images or image selections.

Chapter Four

Covers

Filters – an overview

Paint Shop Pro provides numerous special filters which you can use to customise images.

You can use filters to:

Enhance image edges

Paint Shop Pro calls these 'Edge' filters and provides

— Edge Enhance
— Edge Enhance More
— Find Edges
— Find Horizontal Edges
— Find Vertical Edges
— Trace Contour

REMEMBER

Filters can be regarded as mini-programs built into Paint Shop Pro which alter the characteristics of individual pixels based on the relationship between:

- the current colour
- neighbouring colours

Blur/sharpen images

Paint Shop Pro calls these 'Normal' filters and provides

— Blur
— Blur More
— Soften
— Soften More
— Sharpen
— Sharpen More
— Unsharpen

HANDY TIP

Experiment with applying more than one filter to images (or the same filter more than once) – the effects can be dramatic.

Apply miscellaneous effects

Paint Shop Pro calls these 'Special' filters and provides:

— Add Noise
— Despeckle
— Dilate
— Emboss
— Erode
— Median
— Mosaic

You can also create – and apply – your own filters.

...contd

REMEMBER

Filters work with the following image types:

- coloured images with more than 256 colours
- 256-colour greyscales

If the image you want to apply a filter to doesn't meet these criteria, carry out the relevant procedure in the HANDY TIP on page 183.

You can apply filters in two ways:

- via a menu

- via the Filter Browser

Both techniques are easy and convenient to use, but for most filters (where there is no intermediary dialog which allows you to specify filter settings), the Filter Browser is especially useful.

The Filter Browser

The Filter Browser is a special dialog which lets you preview the effects of applying a filter *before* you commit yourself to doing so.

It's also a way of accessing *every* available filter, without having to pull down a succession of menus.

In the following illustration, the Filter Browser is previewing the effect of applying the Trace Contour filter:

Filter effects are previewed here

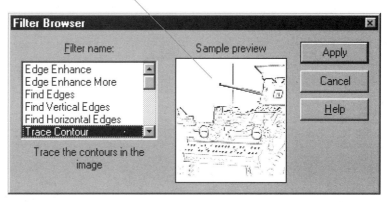

The Edge Enhance filter

Use the Edge Enhance filter to increase image clarity.

The illustration below shows an image *before* the Edge Ehance filter has been applied:

And now the result of applying the filter:

Using the Edge Enhance filter

If you only want to apply the filter to a part of the image, define the appropriate selection area first.

Use either of the following methods to launch the Edge Enhance filter:

The menu route

Pull down the Image menu and do the following:

Click here

2 Click here

In version 3, the Image menu is slightly different.

The Browser route

Pull down the Image menu and click Filter Browser. Now do the following:

Click here

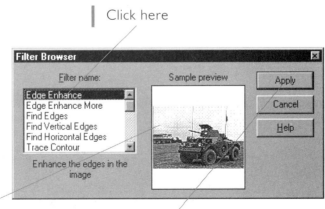

The effect of applying the chosen filter is previewed here:

2 Click here

The Edge Enhance More filter

Use the Edge Enhance More filter to increase image clarity even more.

The illustration below shows an image *before* the filter has been applied:

And now the result of applying the filter:

Notice that the Edge Enhance More filter has an even stronger effect.

Using the Edge Enhance More filter

If you only want to apply the filter to a part of the image, define the appropriate selection area first.

In version 3, the Image menu is slightly different.

Use the Edge Enhance More filter to increase image clarity even more than the Edge Enhance filter. Use either of the following methods:

The menu route

Pull down the Image menu and do the following:

Click here

2 Click here

The Browser route

Pull down the Image menu and click Filter Browser. Now do the following:

Click here

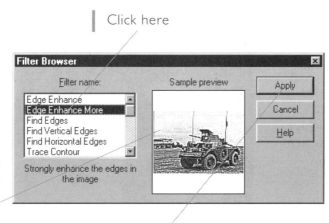

The effect of applying the chosen filter is previewed here:

2 Click here

The Find Edges filter

Use the Find Edges filter when you need to identify – and emphasise – those parts of an image which have significant colour transitions.

The illustration below shows an image *before* the filter has been applied:

And now the result of applying the filter:

 The Find Edges filter produces results which are dramatically creative.

Using the Find Edges filter

If you only want to apply the filter to a part of the image, define the appropriate selection area first.

In version 3, the Image menu is slightly different.

Use either of the following methods to launch the Find Edges filter:

The menu route

Pull down the Image menu and do the following:

Click here

2 Click here

The Browser route

Pull down the Image menu and click Filter Browser. Now do the following:

Click here

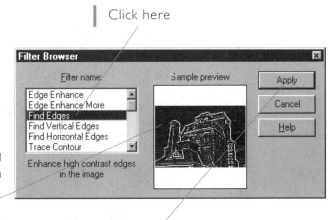

The effect of applying the chosen filter is previewed here:

2 Click here

The Horizontal Edges filter

Use the Find Horizontal Edges filter when you need to identify – and emphasise – those parts of an image which have significant horizontal colour transitions.

The illustration below shows an image *before* the filter has been applied:

And now the result of applying the filter:

The Find Horizontal Edges filter produces results which are similar to the Find Edges filter, and just as dramatically creative.

HANDY TIP

Using the Horizontal Edges filter

Use either of the following methods to launch the Find Horizontal Edges filter:

If you only want to apply the filter to a part of the image, define the appropriate selection area first.

The menu route

Pull down the Image menu and do the following:

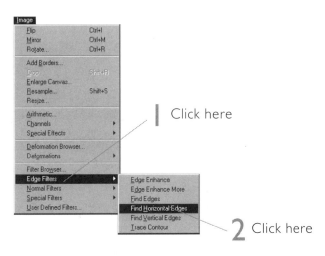

Click here

2 Click here

In version 3, the Image menu is slightly different.

The Browser route

Pull down the Image menu and click Filter Browser. Now do the following:

Click here

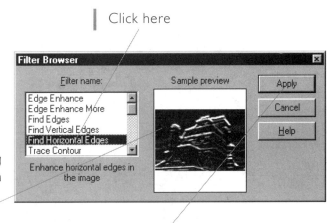

The effect of applying the chosen filter is previewed here:

2 Click here

The Vertical Edges filter

Use the Find Vertical Edges filter when you need to identify – and emphasise – those parts of an image which have significant vertical colour transitions.

The illustration below shows an image *before* the filter has been applied:

And now the result of applying the filter:

HANDY TIP

The Find Vertical Edges filter produces results which are similar to the Find Edges filter, and just as dramatically creative.

Using the Vertical Edges filter

HANDY TIP

If you only want to apply the filter to a part of the image, define the appropriate selection area first.

REMEMBER

In version 3, the Image menu is slightly different.

Use either of the following methods to launch the Find Vertical Edges filter:

The menu route

Pull down the Image menu and do the following:

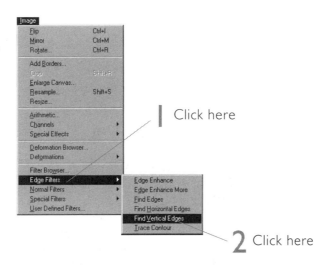

Click here

2 Click here

The Browser route

Pull down the Image menu and click Filter Browser. Now do the following:

Click here

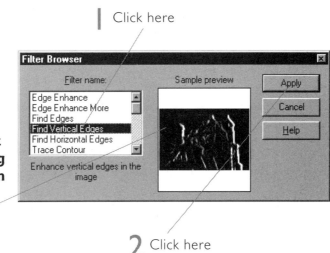

HANDY TIP

The effect of applying the chosen filter is previewed here:

2 Click here

The Trace Contour filter

The Trace Contour filter is a specialist edge filter which, effectively, outlines images by defining a border around them.

The illustration below shows an image *before* the Trace Contour filter has been applied:

And now the result of applying the filter:

Using the Trace Contour filter

If you only want to apply the filter to a part of the image, define the appropriate selection area first.

Use either of the following methods to launch the Trace Contour filter:

The menu route
Pull down the Image menu and do the following:

In version 3, the Image menu is slightly different.

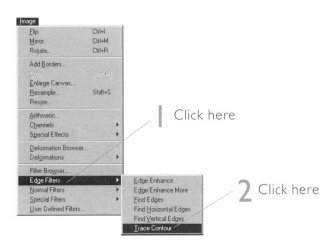

Click here

2 Click here

The Browser route
Pull down the Image menu and click Filter Browser. Now do the following:

Click here

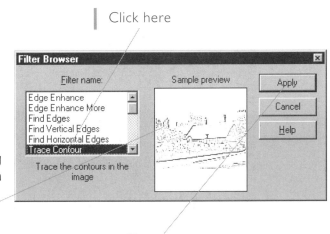

The effect of applying the chosen filter is previewed here:

2 Click here

The ßlur filter

The Blur filter lightens pixels which adjoin the hard edges of defined lines and shaded areas, making for a hazy effect.

The illustration below shows an image *before* the Blur filter has been applied:

And now the result of applying the filter:

Using the Blur filter

 If you only want to apply the filter to a part of the image, define the appropriate selection area first.

Use either of the following methods to launch the Blur filter:

The menu route

Pull down the Image menu and do the following:

 In version 3, the Image menu is slightly different.

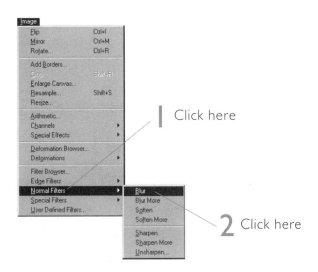

Click here

2 Click here

The Browser route

Pull down the Image menu and click Filter Browser. Now do the following:

Click here

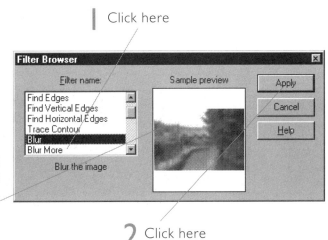

 The effect of applying the chosen filter is previewed here:

2 Click here

The ßlur More filter

The Blur More filter produces an effect which is similar to, but considerably stronger than, the Blur filter.

The illustration below shows an image *before* the Blur More filter has been applied:

And now the result of applying the filter:

Using the Blur More filter

If you only want to apply the filter to a part of the image, define the appropriate selection area first.

Use either of the following methods to launch the Blur More filter:

The menu route
Pull down the Image menu and do the following:

In version 3, the Image menu is slightly different.

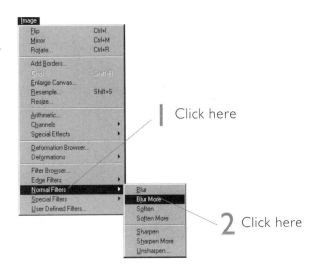

Click here

2 Click here

The Browser route
Pull down the Image menu and click Filter Browser. Now do the following:

Click here

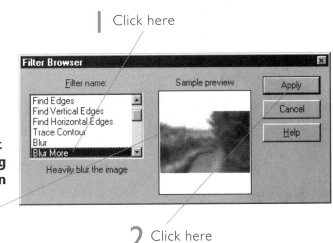

The effect of applying the chosen filter is previewed here:

2 Click here

The Soften filter

The Soften filter smooths out an image by decreasing the contrast between neighbouring pixels.

The illustration below shows an image *before* the Soften filter has been applied:

And now the result of applying the filter to a selection area within the image:

See the magnified view of part of the selection area.

Using the Soften filter

HANDY TIP

If you only want to apply the filter to a part of the image, define the appropriate selection area first.

Use either of the following methods to launch the Soften filter:

The menu route
Pull down the Image menu and do the following:

REMEMBER

In version 3, the Image menu is slightly different.

Click here

2 Click here

The Browser route
Pull down the Image menu and click Filter Browser. Now do the following:

Click here

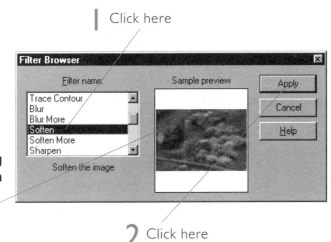
HANDY TIP

The effect of applying the chosen filter is previewed here:

2 Click here

The Soften More filter

The Soften More filter produces an effect which is similar to, but considerably stronger than, the Soften filter.

The illustration below shows an image *before* the Soften More filter has been applied:

And now the result of applying the filter:

Using the Soften More filter

If you only want to apply the filter to a part of the image, define the appropriate selection area first.

In version 3, the Image menu is slightly different.

Use either of the following methods to launch the Soften More filter:

The menu route
Pull down the Image menu and do the following:

Click here

2 Click here

The Browser route
Pull down the Image menu and click Filter Browser. Now do the following:

Click here

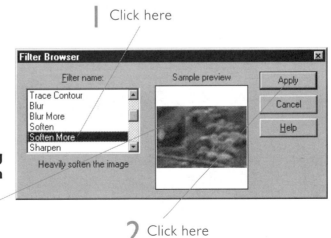

The effect of applying the chosen filter is previewed here:

2 Click here

The Sharpen filter

The Sharpen filter improves an image's focus and clarity.

The illustration below shows an image *before* the Sharpen filter has been applied:

And now the result of applying the filter:

Using the Sharpen filter

If you only want to apply the filter to a part of the image, define the appropriate selection area first.

In version 3, the Image menu is slightly different.

Use either of the following methods to launch the Sharpen filter:

The menu route
Pull down the Image menu and do the following:

Click here

2 Click here

The Browser route
Pull down the Image menu and click Filter Browser. Now do the following:

Click here

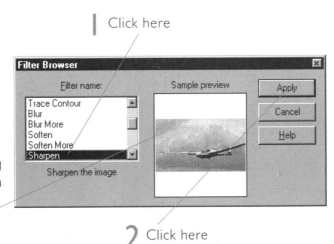

2 Click here

The effect of applying the chosen filter is previewed here:

The Sharpen More filter

The Sharpen More filter produces an effect which is similar to, but considerably stronger than, the Sharpen filter.

The illustration below shows an image *before* the Sharpen More filter has been applied:

HANDY TIP

You can also sharpen images (though in a different way) by using the paradoxically named Unsharpen filter.

Pull down the Image menu and click Normal Filters, Unsharpen. In the Unsharpen dialog, adjust the settings in the Clipping and Strength fields appropriately.

Click OK to apply your changes.

And now the result of applying the filter:

Using the Sharpen More filter

If you only want to apply the filter to a part of the image, define the appropriate selection area first.

In version 3, the Image menu is slightly different.

Use either of the following methods to launch the Sharpen More filter:

The menu route
Pull down the Image menu and do the following:

Click here

2 Click here

The Browser route
Pull down the Image menu and click Filter Browser. Now do the following:

Click here

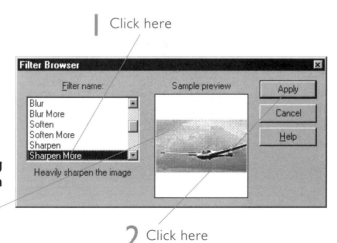

2 Click here

The effect of applying the chosen filter is previewed here:

The Add Noise filter

The Add Noise filter ensures that images have randomly distributed colour pixels; you can determine, in a special dialog, the extent and type of the distribution.

The illustration below shows an image *before* the Add Noise filter has been applied:

And now the result of applying the filter:

 The Add Noise filter produces creative effects which would otherwise be very difficult and time-consuming to achieve.

Using the Add Noise filter

HANDY TIP

If you only want to apply the filter to a part of the image, define the appropriate selection area first.

Use either of the following methods to launch the Add Noise filter:

The menu route

Pull down the Image menu and click Special Filters, Add Noise. Now carry out the following steps:

REMEMBER

Re. step 2 – the permitted range is:

| 1 | almost no noise |
| 100 | maximum noise |

| Select a distribution method

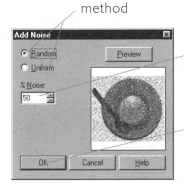

2 Specify a noise %

3 Click here

HANDY TIP

In the case of the Add Noise filter, using the menu route has one advantage: you can specify the degree to which the filter is applied.

The Browser route

Pull down the Image menu and click Filter Browser. Now do the following:

| Click one of these

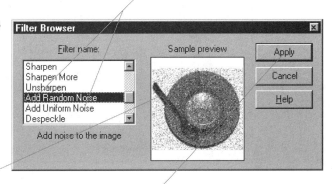

HANDY TIP

The effect of applying the chosen filter is previewed here:

2 Click here

The Despeckle filter

The Despeckle filter blurs all of an image except those locations (edges) where meaningful colour changes take place.

The illustration below shows an image *before* the Despeckle filter has been applied:

And now the result of applying the filter:

Notice how the Despeckle filter blurs the contents of the magnifying lens.

Using the Despeckle filter

If you only want to apply the filter to a part of the image, define the appropriate selection area first.

In version 3, the Image menu is slightly different.

Use either of the following methods to launch the Despeckle filter:

The menu route

Pull down the Image menu and do the following:

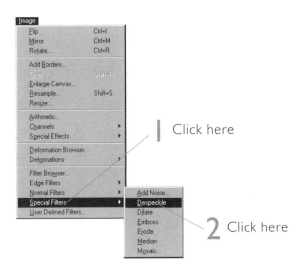

Click here

2 Click here

The Browser route

Pull down the Image menu and click Filter Browser. Now do the following:

Click here

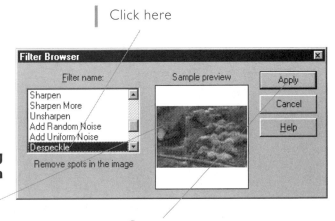

The effect of applying the chosen filter is previewed here:

2 Click here

The Dilate filter

The Dilate filter enhances light areas in an image.

The illustration below shows an image *before* the Dilate filter has been applied:

And now the result of applying the filter:

Using the Dilate filter

If you only want to apply the filter to a part of the image, define the appropriate selection area first.

Use either of the following methods to launch the Dilate filter:

The menu route

Pull down the Image menu and do the following:

In version 3, the Image menu is slightly different.

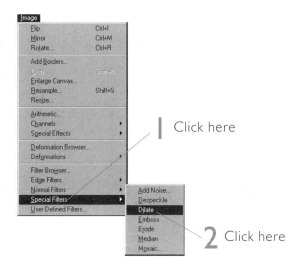

Click here

2 Click here

The Browser route

Pull down the Image menu and click Filter Browser. Now do the following:

Click here

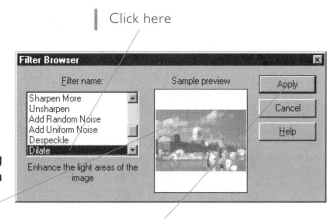

The effect of applying the chosen filter is previewed here:

2 Click here

The Emboss filter

The Emboss filter suppresses colour within an image and outlines it with black; this creates a raised effect.

The illustration below shows an image *before* the Emboss filter has been applied:

And now the result of applying the filter:

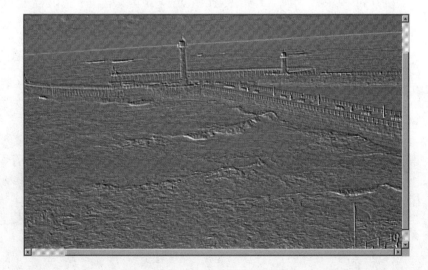

Using the Emboss filter

HANDY TIP

If you only want to apply the filter to a part of the image, define the appropriate selection area first.

REMEMBER

In version 3, the Image menu is slightly different.

Use either of the following methods to launch the Emboss filter:

The menu route

Pull down the Image menu and do the following:

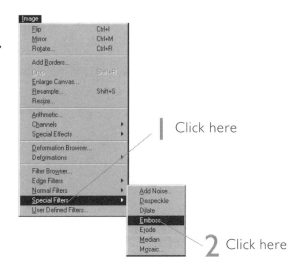

Click here

2 Click here

The Browser route

Pull down the Image menu and click Filter Browser. Now do the following:

Click here

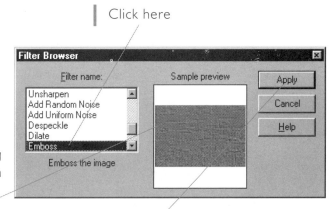

HANDY TIP

The effect of applying the chosen filter is previewed here:

2 Click here

The Erode filter

The Erode filter emphasises dark areas in an image.

The illustration below shows an image *before* the Erode filter has been applied:

And now the result of applying the filter:

Using the Erode filter

If you only want to apply the filter to a part of the image, define the appropriate selection area first.

In version 3, the Image menu is slightly different.

Use either of the following methods to launch the Erode filter:

The menu route

Pull down the Image menu and do the following:

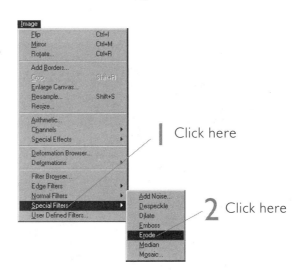

Click here

2 Click here

The Browser route

Pull down the Image menu and click Filter Browser. Now do the following:

Click here

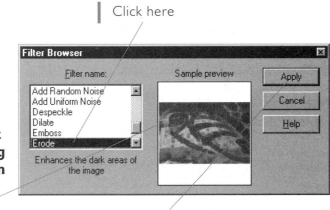

The effect of applying the chosen filter is previewed here:

2 Click here

The Median filter

The Median filter reduces image noise by 'averaging' pixel brightness and discarding pixels which have relatively little in common with their neighbours.

The illustration below shows an image *before* the Median filter has been applied:

And now the result of applying the filter:

Notice how the Median filter blurs the contents of the magnifying lens.

Using the Median filter

If you only want to apply the filter to a part of the image, define the appropriate selection area first.

In version 3, the Image menu is slightly different.

Use either of the following methods to launch the Median filter:

The menu route
Pull down the Image menu and do the following:

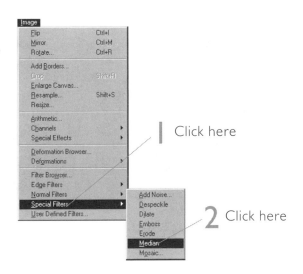

Click here

2 Click here

The Browser route
Pull down the Image menu and click Filter Browser. Now do the following:

Click here

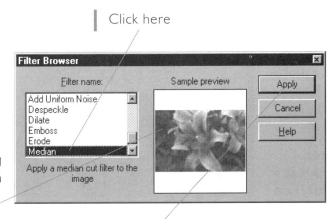

2 Click here

HANDY TIP

The effect of applying the chosen filter is previewed here:

The Mosaic filter

The Mosaic filter groups pixels into blocks, according to the block dimensions you specify.

The illustration below shows an image *before* the Mosaic filter has been applied:

And now one possible result of applying the filter:

 This effect was achieved with the following settings in the Mosaic dialog (see page 135):

20	Block Width
20	Block Height

Using higher settings produces a much more marked effect.

Using the Mosaic filter

HANDY TIP

If you only want to apply the filter to a part of the image, define the appropriate selection area first.

Use either of the following methods to launch the Mosaic filter:

The menu route

Pull down the Image menu and click Special Filters, Mosaic. Now carry out the following steps:

| Enter a block width

REMEMBER

Re. steps 1 and 2 – the permitted range is:

| 1 | almost no effect |
| 100 | maximum effect |

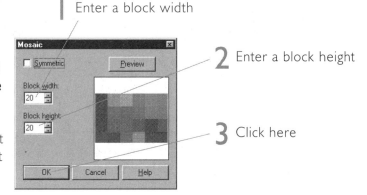

2 Enter a block height

3 Click here

HANDY TIP

In the case of the Median filter, using the menu route has one advantage: you can specify the degree to which the filter is applied.

The Browser route

Pull down the Image menu and click Filter Browser. Now do the following:

| Click here

HANDY TIP

The effect of applying the chosen filter is previewed here:

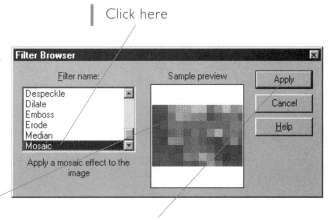

2 Click here

User-defined filters

You can define your own filters, easily and conveniently. Once created, new filters can be named, saved and applied to images whenever required.

The next illustration shows an image *before* the application of a user-defined filter:

And now the result of applying the filter to a circular selection area:

Creating filters

Defining your own filter

Pull down the Image menu and click User Defined Filters. Now carry out the following steps:

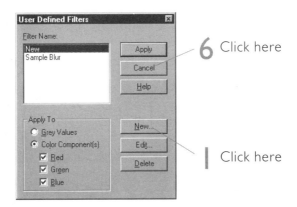

6 Click here

| Click here

In version 3, the dialog on the right is slightly different. (For instance, only a 5 x 5 matrix is supported.)

2 Name the new filter

3 Type in the appropriate (whole) values

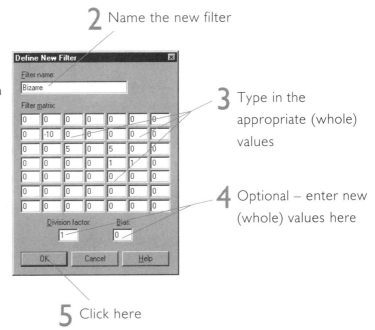

The settings shown here produce the effect demonstrated on page 136.

4 Optional – enter new (whole) values here

5 Click here

Applying user-defined filters

Do the following to apply filters you've created:

Applying your own filters

First, open the image you want to apply the filter to. (Then, if applicable, define a selection area to limit the effect of the filter). Now carry out the following steps:

 To edit an existing user-defined filter, follow steps 1-2 on the right. Instead of carrying out step 3, click this button:

In the Edit User Defined Filter dialog, make the relevant adjustments in line with steps 3-4 on page 137. Click OK. Click Cancel (or follow step 3 if you want to apply the amended filter immediately).

Click here

 In version 3, the dialog on the right is slightly different.

2 Click a user-defined filter

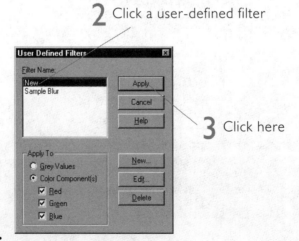

3 Click here

Chapter Five

Deformations and effects

In this chapter, you'll add creative effects to images or image selections. You'll do this by applying Paint Shop Pro's numerous deformations. Finally, version 4 users will apply special effects to images, selections or masks.

Covers

Deformations/effects – an overview

In addition to the filters discussed in chapter 4, Paint Shop Pro also offers:

- a further series of filters (called deformations) which distort images

- (in the case of version 4 only) a range of special effects – see pages 158-168

The additional filters are:

— Circle

— Cylinder - Horizontal

— Cylinder - Vertical

— Motion Blur

— Pentagon

— Perspective - Horizontal

— Perspective - Vertical

— Pinch

— Punch

— Skew

— Wind

The special effects are:

— Add Drop Shadow

— Create Seamless Pattern

— Cutout

— Chisel

— Buttonize

— Hot Wax Coating

Experiment with applying more than one deformation or effect to images (or the same deformation/effect more than once) – the results can be dramatic.

...contd

 Images must fall into the following categories:

- coloured images with more than 256 colours
- 256-colour greyscales

for deformations and special effects to work on them.
If the image you want to apply a deformation to doesn't meet these criteria, carry out the relevant procedure in the HANDY TIP on page 183.

 Special effects cannot be applied via a Browser.

You can apply deformations in two ways:

- via a menu

- via the Deformation Browser

Both techniques are easy and convenient to use, but for most deformations (where there is no intermediary dialog which allows you to specify deformation settings), the Deformation Browser is especially useful.

The Deformation Browser

The Deformation Browser is a special dialog which lets you preview the effects of applying a deformation *before* you commit yourself to doing so.

It's also a way of accessing *every* available deformation, without having to pull down a succession of menus.

In the following illustration, the Deformation Browser is previewing the effect of applying the Skew deformation:

Deformations are previewed here

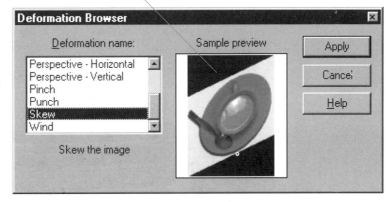

The Circle deformation

The Circle deformation produces a 'fish-eye' effect.

The illustration below shows an image *before* the Circle deformation has been applied:

In version 3, you can only apply this deformation to *whole* images, not selection areas.

And now the result of applying the deformation:

Using the Circle deformation

HANDY TIP

In version 4, if you want to limit the effect to a part of the image, define the appropriate selection area first.

REMEMBER

In version 3, the Image menu is slightly different.

Use either of the following methods to launch the Circle deformation:

The menu route
Pull down the Image menu and do the following:

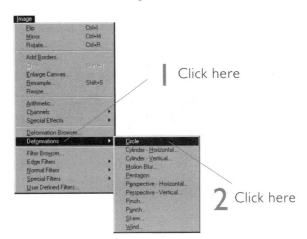

Click here

2 Click here

The Browser route
Pull down the Image menu and click Deformation Browser. Now do the following:

Click here

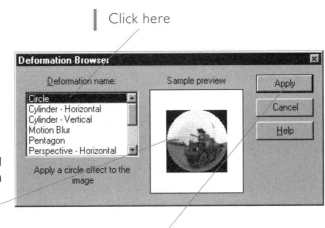

HANDY TIP

The result of applying the chosen effect is previewed here:

2 Click here

The Cylinder deformations

Of the two cylinder deformations, the Cylinder - Horizontal deformation stretches an image horizontally, while the Cylinder - Vertical deformation stretches it vertically.

See the examples below:

The original image

After applying the Cylinder - Horizontal deformation

After applying the Cylinder - Vertical deformation

Using the Cylinder deformations

If you want to limit the effect to a part of the image, define the appropriate selection area first.

Use the following methods to launch either of the Cylinder deformations:

The menu route

Pull down the Image menu and click Deformations, Cylinder - Horizontal or Deformations, Cylinder - Vertical. Now carry out the following steps:

Type in a % effect

2 Click here

Re. step 2 – the permitted range is:

| 1 | almost no effect |
| 100 | maximum effect |

In the case of these effects, using the menu route has one advantage: you can specify the degree to which the deformation is applied.

The Browser route

Pull down the Image menu and click Deformation Browser. Now do the following:

Click one of these

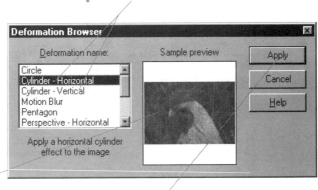

The result of applying the chosen effect is previewed here:

2 Click here

The Motion Blur deformation

The Motion Blur deformation produces a blurred effect.

The illustration below shows an image *before* the Motion Blur deformation has been applied:

And now the result of applying the deformation:

Using the Motion Blur deformation

HANDY TIP

If you want to limit the effect to a part of the image, define the appropriate selection area first.

Use either of the following methods to launch the Motion Blur deformation:

The menu route

Pull down the Image menu and click Deformations, Motion Blur. Now carry out the following steps:

HANDY TIP

Version 3 users should omit steps 1-3 (the Motion Blur dialog does not launch). Instead, the deformation is applied immediately.

Type in an angle

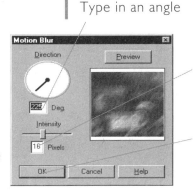

2 Type in a pixel limit

3 Click here

The Browser route

Pull down the Image menu and click Deformation Browser. Now do the following:

REMEMBER

Re. step 2 above – the permitted range is:

| | almost no effect |
| 40 | maximum effect |

Click here

HANDY TIP

The result of applying the chosen effect is previewed here:

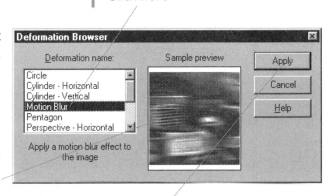

2 Click here

The Pentagon deformation

The Pentagon deformation forces an image into a pentagon.

The illustration below shows an image *before* the Pentagon deformation has been applied:

In version 3, you can only apply this deformation to *whole* images, not selection areas.

And now the result of applying the deformation:

Using the Pentagon deformation

In version 4, if you want to limit the effect to a part of the image, define the appropriate selection area first.

Use either of the following methods to launch the Pentagon deformation:

The menu route
Pull down the Image menu and do the following:

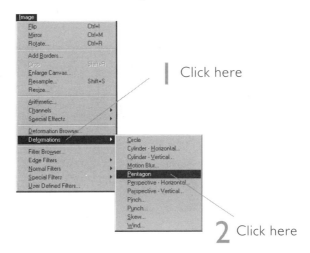

Click here

2 Click here

In version 3, the Image menu is slightly different.

The Browser route
Pull down the Image menu and click Deformation Browser. Now do the following:

Click here

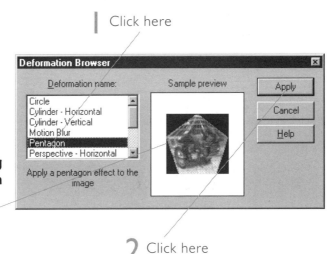

2 Click here

The result of applying the chosen effect is previewed here:

The Perspective deformations

There are two perspective deformations. The Perspective - Horizontal deformation slants an image horizontally, while the Perspective - Vertical deformations slants it vertically. The result incorporates a perspective effect.

See the examples below:

REMEMBER

In version 3, you can only apply this deformation to *whole* **images, not selection areas.**

The original image

After applying the Perspective - Horizontal deformation

After applying the Perspective - Vertical deformation

Using the Perspective deformations

HANDY TIP

In version 4, if you want to limit the effect to a part of the image, define the appropriate selection area first.

Use the following methods to launch either of the Perspective deformations:

The menu route

Pull down the Image menu and click Deformations, Perspective - Horizontal or Deformations, Perspective - Vertical. Now carry out the following steps:

Type in a % effect

2 Click here

REMEMBER

Re. step 1 – the permitted range is:

1   almost no effect
100   maximum effect

HANDY TIP

In the case of these effects, using the menu route has one advantage: you can specify the degree to which the deformation is applied.

The Browser route

Pull down the Image menu and click Deformation Browser. Now do the following:

Click one of these

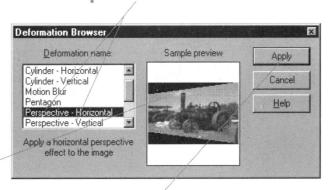

2 Click here

HANDY TIP

The result of applying the chosen effect is previewed here:

The Punch deformation

The Punch deformation expands images from the centre.

The illustration below shows an image *before* the Punch deformation has been applied:

And now the result of applying the deformation:

Using the Punch deformation

If you want to limit the effect to a part of the image, define the appropriate selection area first.

Use either of the following methods to launch the Punch deformation:

The menu route

Pull down the Image menu and click Deformations, Punch. Now carry out the following steps:

Type in a % effect

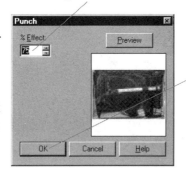

2 Click here

Re. step 1 – the permitted range is:

| 1 | almost no effect |
| 100 | maximum effect |

The Browser route

In the case of this effect, using the menu route has one advantage: you can specify the degree to which the deformation is applied.

Pull down the Image menu and click Deformation Browser. Now do the following:

Click here

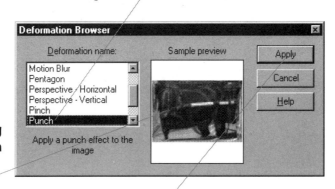

The result of applying the chosen effect is previewed here:

2 Click here

The Skew deformation

The Skew deformation slants images to the left or right.

The illustration below shows an image *before* the Skew deformation has been applied:

In version 3, you can only apply this deformation to *whole* images, not selection areas.

And now the result of applying the deformation:

Skewing has a dramatic effect on images. This is a moderate skew (only 10% – see steps 1 and 2 on page 155).

Using the Skew deformation

In version 4, if you want to limit the effect to a part of the image, define the appropriate selection area first.

Use either of the following methods to launch the Skew deformation:

The menu route

Pull down the Image menu and click Deformations, Skew. Now carry out step 1 OR step 2. Finally, perform step 3:

| Type in a horizontal skew %

Re. steps 1 and 2 – the permitted range is:

| 1 | almost no effect |
| 45 | maximum effect |

2 Type in a vertical skew %

3 Click here

In the case of this effect, using the menu route has one advantage: you can specify the degree to which the deformation is applied.

The Browser route

Pull down the Image menu and click Deformation Browser. Now do the following:

| Click here

The result of applying the chosen effect is previewed here:

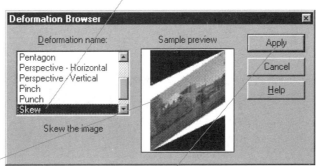

2 Click here

The Wind deformation

The Wind deformation inserts horizontal (very thin) lines into images, an effect which mimics wind.

The illustration below shows an image *before* the Wind deformation has been applied:

And now the result of applying the deformation:

Using the Wind deformation

If you want to limit the effect to a part of the image, define the appropriate selection area first.

Use either of the following methods to launch the Wind deformation:

The menu route

Pull down the Image menu and click Deformations, Wind. Now carry out the following steps:

Re. step 2 – the permitted range is:

| 1 | almost no effect |
| 20 | maximum effect |

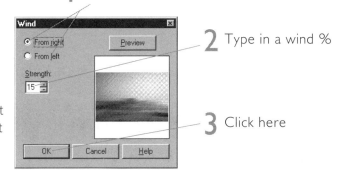

Choose a direction

2 Type in a wind %

3 Click here

In the case of this effect, using the menu route has one advantage: you can specify the degree to which the deformation is applied.

The Browser route

Pull down the Image menu and click Deformation Browser. Now do the following:

Click here

The result of applying the chosen effect is previewed here:

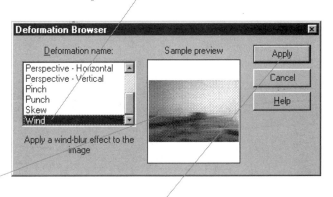

2 Click here

The Drop Shadow effect

You can have Paint Shop Pro surround images with a shadow effect.

The illustration below shows an image *before* the Drop Shadow effect has been applied:

 HANDY TIP

Special effects can only be applied in version 4 of Paint Shop Pro.

 HANDY TIP

This effect can only be applied to selection areas.

And now the result of applying the effect:

 HANDY TIP

If you want to drop-shadow an entire image, you have to:

1. press Shift+A to select the entire image
2. increase the image's canvas appropriately (see pages 16-17)

Drop shadow

Using the Drop Shadow effect

First define a selection area. (If you select an entire image, also increase the image canvas). Then pull down the Image menu and do the following:

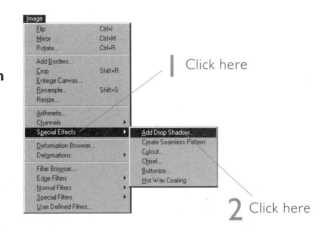

In version 3, the Image menu is slightly different.

| Click here

2 Click here

3 Click here; select a shadow colour

Re. step 4 – the permitted range is:

0 maximum sharpness

9 maximum blur

4 Enter a blur setting

5 Enter an opacity

Re. step 5 – the permitted range is:

| almost transparent

255 completely opaque

6 Type in shadow dimensions

7 Click here

The Create Seamless Pattern effect

You can have Paint Shop Pro 4 convert a selection area into a pattern. Once the pattern has been created, it can be inserted seamlessly into another image as a pattern fill. (See pages 86-87 for how to use pattern fills).

The illustration below shows an image complete with selection area:

Special effects can only be applied in version 4 of Paint Shop Pro.

Selection area

This effect can only be applied to selection areas.

And below, the selection area converted into a pattern:

Creating a seamless pattern

First define a selection area. Then pull down the Image menu and do the following:

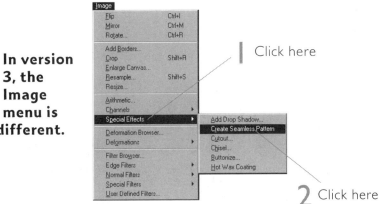

REMEMBER

In version 3, the Image menu is slightly different.

Click here

1

2 Click here

Paint Shop Pro 4 now creates the seamless pattern.

Caveat

If the selection area you've defined is too close to one or more image edges, Paint Shop Pro launches a special message. Carry out the following additional step:

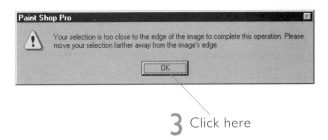

3 Click here

Now do ONE of the following:

1.   Move the selection area to another location

2.   Define another (smaller) selection area

The Cutout effect

You can have Paint Shop Pro 4 convert a selection area into a 'cutout'. You then have the impression of looking through the overall image to a recessed surface.

The illustration below shows an image *before* the Cutout effect has been applied:

Special effects can only be applied in version 4 of Paint Shop Pro.

Selection area

This effect can only be applied to selection areas.

And below, the selection area converted into a (greyscale) cutout:

You can elect to have the cutout:
- filled with colour
or
- filled with the underlying image

Using the Cutout effect

First define a selection area. Then pull down the Image menu and do the following:

In version 3, the Image menu is slightly different.

If you want the cutout to be filled with a colour, click Fill interior with color in the dialog on the right. Then click the arrow to the right of the Interior color field and select a colour in the list.

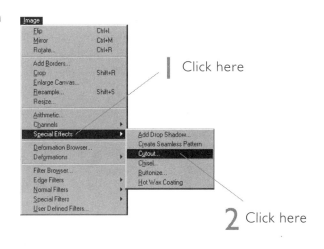

1 Click here

2 Click here

3 Click here; select a shadow colour

Re. step 4 – the permitted range is:

0   maximum sharpness

9   maximum blur

Re. step 5 – the permitted range is:

1   almost transparent

255 completely opaque

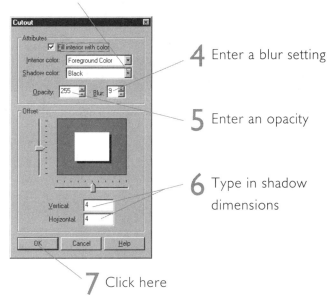

4 Enter a blur setting

5 Enter an opacity

6 Type in shadow dimensions

7 Click here

The Chisel effect

The Chisel special effect makes the defined selection area appear to have been carved out of stone.

The illustration below shows sample text *before* the Chisel effect has been applied:

 Special effects can only be applied in version 4 of Paint Shop Pro.

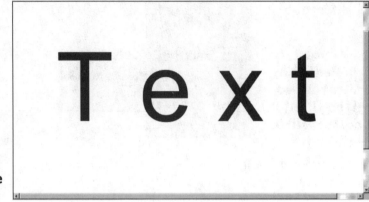

 This effect can only be applied to selection areas.

And now the result of applying the effect:

 Use the Magic Wand tool to select a letter. Then follow steps 1-5 on page 165 to apply the chisel effect.
  Repeat this process for each letter.

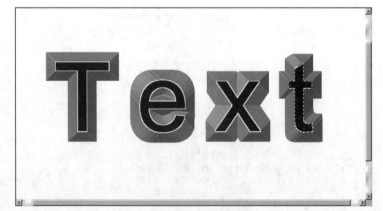

Using the Chisel effect

First define a selection area. Then pull down the Image menu and do the following:

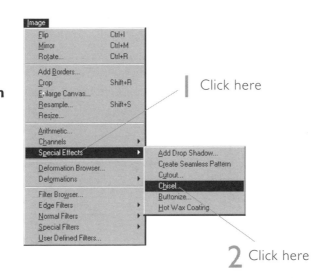

Click here

2 Click here

In version 3, the Image menu is slightly different.

Re. step 3 – the permitted range is:

1-100

measured in pixels. (72 pixels are roughly equal to one inch).

Re. step 4 – this determines whether the chisel border is transparent, or uses the background colour.

3 Type in a size

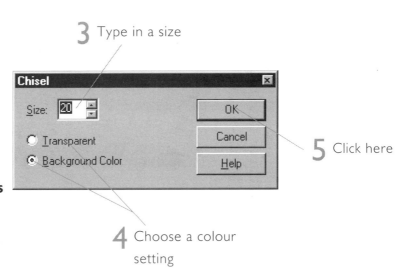

5 Click here

4 Choose a colour setting

The Buttonize effect

The Buttonize special effect applies a raised, 3D border.

The illustration below shows a selected, outlined rectangle *before* the Buttonize effect has been applied:

Special effects can only be applied in version 4 of Paint Shop Pro.

And below, the selection area converted into a button:

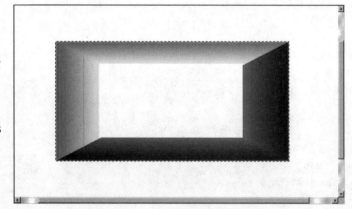

This effect can be applied to selection areas, entire images or masks.

Using the Buttonize effect

See chapter 6 for how to work with masks.

If appropriate, define a selection area or a mask. (Do neither if you want to affect the entire image). Then pull down the Image menu and do the following:

In version 3, the Image menu is slightly different.

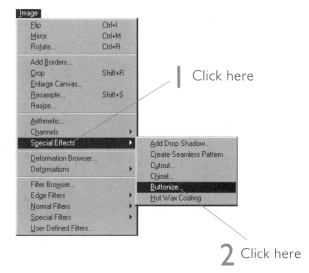

Click here

2 Click here

Re. step 3 – the permitted range is: 1-50 **measured as a percentage of the button size.**

3 Type in a size

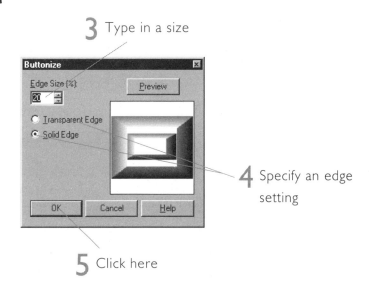

4 Specify an edge setting

5 Click here

The Hot Wax Coating effect

The Hot Wax Coating effect simulates dipping images (or selection areas/masks) in hot wax. Paint Shop Pro uses the current foreground colour in applying the wax effect.

The illustration below shows an image *after* the Hot Wax Coating effect has been applied:

 Here, the Hot Wax Coating effect has been applied with the foreground colour as white.

Applying the Hot Wax Coating effect

 See chapter 6 for how to work with masks.

First, follow the procedures on pages 28-29 to select the appropriate foreground colour. If you want to restrict the effect to part of the active image, define the appropriate selection area or mask. Pull down the Image menu and do the following:

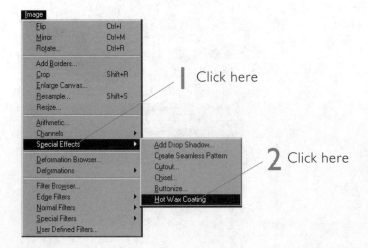

Click here

2 Click here

Advanced techniques

In this chapter, you'll learn how to apply borders to images; carry out screen captures; and apply/edit masks. Then you'll crop images; work with histograms to readjust colour values; and carry out other colour corrections (including Posterize and Solarize). Finally, you'll preview – and print – your work.

Chapter Six

Covers

Advanced techniques – an overview

Paint Shop Pro lets you carry out a wide assortment of advanced operations. You can:

- border images very easily and conveniently

- capture Windows screens or screen components (and save them to disk as graphics files)

- create masks (advanced selections which, in some ways, resemble stencils), and save them to disk for later use

- crop images (cropping is the removal of those sections of an image which are not required, and involves the use of rectangular selections)

- carry out colour corrections. This involves:

  — viewing histograms (graphs displaying colour and luminance distribution)

  — using the histogram functions Equalize and Stretch

- convert colour images to greyscale

- invert ('negative') images

- customise other colour functions e.g. brightness/ contrast and highlight/shadow

- Posterize images

- Solarize images

- preview images before printing

- print images

Bordering images

You can have Paint Shop Pro surround images with a border; this is defined with the current foreground colour. You can have each edge bordered automatically, or you can specify which edges should be affected.

Applying a border

HANDY TIP

If you want each border to be the same, click here: and omit step 1. Now complete *one* of the edge fields. Finally, follow step 2.

Open the image you wish to border. Use the techniques discussed on pages 28-29 to select the appropriate foreground colour. Pull down the Image menu and click Add Borders. Now do the following:

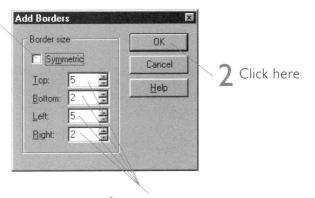

2 Click here

Type in border measurements

The illustration below shows an image with an uneven (black) border:

Screen captures

You can have Paint Shop Pro create a snapshot of all or part of any Windows screen.

You can:

Version 3 users can only use a keystroke combination to trigger a capture.

- specify which part of the screen is captured

- specify the signal which initiates the capture. You can use:

   — a keystroke combination (known as a 'hotkey') – e.g. F I I or Alt+Ctrl+F I

   — the right mouse button

- include the cursor in the capture

Having Paint Shop Pro perform a screen capture consists of the following sequential stages:

A. arranging the screen appropriately (this includes making the program whose screen you want to capture active)

B. switching to Paint Shop Pro

C. telling Paint Shop Pro to initiate a capture (at which point it minimises)

Paint Shop Pro was used to perform all of the screen captures in this book.

D. issuing the capture signal

E. returning to Paint Shop Pro (the captured screen automatically occupies its own window) and performing any necessary editing actions e.g. cropping or converting to greyscale)

F. using standard procedures to save the screen capture as a graphics file for later use

...contd

HANDY TIP Version 3 users should perform steps A-B on page 172, then omit the procedures on the right. Instead, do the following:

1. Pull down the Capture menu and click Hot Key Setup. Select a keystroke. Click OK.
2. Optional – to capture the cursor, pull down the Capture menu and click Include Cursor.
3. Pull down the Capture menu again and select a region.

Paint Shop Pro minimises. Now follow the relevant procedures on the right – with one exception. If you selected Area in the Capture menu, double-click with the left mouse button where you want the area to begin. Drag to define the area. Releasing the button initiates the capture.

Performing a screen capture

Perform steps A and B on page 172. Now pull down the Capture menu and click Setup. Do the following:

1 Select a region   2 Optional – select a trigger

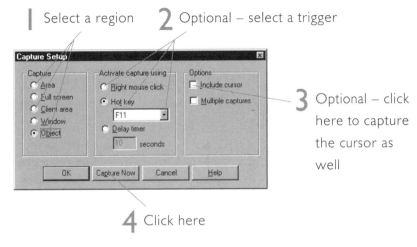

3 Optional – click here to capture the cursor as well

4 Click here

Paint Shop Pro minimises, and you're returned to the application whose screen you want to capture. Now perform ONE of the following:

If you selected Area, Object, Window or Client area in step 1	Place the cursor over the screen component you want to capture
If you selected Full Screen in step 1	Place the cursor anywhere on the screen

Follow step D on page 172. Additionally, if you selected Area in step 1 above, position the cursor at one corner of the area you want to capture; left-click once. Place the cursor at the opposing corner and left-click again.

Back in Paint Shop Pro, perform steps E and F on page 172, as appropriate.

Masks – an overview

You can use the following tools with masks:

- the Paintbrush
- the Retouch tool
- the Clone brush
- the Airbrush
- the Fill tool

Masks are 256-colour greyscale bitmaps which are overlaid over the whole of the image you're working with. They contain 'holes'; you perform editing operations on the areas displayed through the gaps. The holes can be created via:

- selection areas

- other images

Alternatively, the mask can be as large as the underlying image.

To an extent, as we've seen, masks can be regarded as stencils. However, also implicit in the above description is the fact that they act as advanced selection areas. For example, you can control the extent to which a mask operates by defining the colour/greyscale content:

— Black completely protects the underlying image from any changes you make

— White allows your changes to have full effect on the underlying image

— Any intervening shade of grey allows a portion of the effect you generate to take effect; the darker the grey, the less the effect

Filters and special effects you can use with masks include:

- colour correction functions
- image inversion
- Posterize/ Solarize
- all deformations and filters
- the Buttonize special effect
- the Hot Wax Coating special effect

Here, a circular selection was converted into a mask, and then embossed

Empty masks

You can create three types of mask:

* 'empty' masks (they overlay all of the underlying image)

* selection masks (formed from, and based on, a pre-defined selection)

* image masks (based on a second image)

Version 3 users should omit steps 1 and 2.
Instead, pull down the Image menu and click Create Empty Mask. Paint Shop Pro 3 opens the mask in a separate window.

Creating an empty mask
Pull down the Masks menu and do the following:

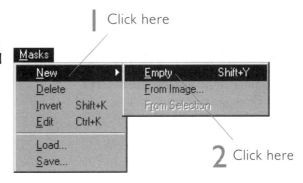

Click here

2 Click here

By default, empty masks are black. In other words, no editing operations will affect them. To alter this, see page 178.

Version 3 users can't follow this procedure.
Instead, empty masks appear in their own windows.
Simply press Ctrl+F6 until the mask window is active.

Viewing an empty mask
To view the mask itself, on top of its underlying image, pull down the View menu and click Through Mask.

An empty mask overlying its image

Selection masks

Selection masks are empty masks which contain a hole (the hole being supplied by the selection area). By default, the area of the mask around the selection is black (i.e. it prevents any effects you apply from working), while the area of the mask within the selection is white (i.e. it gives full rein to any effects).

Creating a selection mask

Define the appropriate selection area (see chapter 2 for how to do this). Pull down the Masks menu and do the following:

Version 3 users should omit steps 1-2.
Instead, pull down the Image menu and click Add Mask. In the Add Mask Channel dialog, ensure Current Selection is activated. Click OK.

Click here

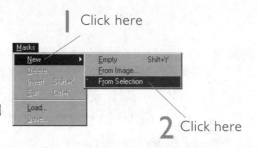

2 Click here

An image complete with circular selection

To achieve this view, version 4 users should choose Through Mask in the View menu.

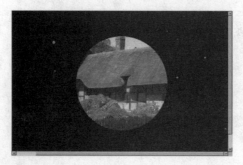

The selection converted to a mask, with part of the underlying image visible

Image masks

Creating masks from other images is a very useful technique. It can produce quite remarkable effects.

Version 3 users should do this slightly differently. Open the host and mask-to-be images, but make the host image active. Pull down the Image menu and click Add Mask. In the Add Mask Channel dialog, click the Source Window arrow; select the image you want to use as a mask. Click OK.

Creating masks from images

Open the image you want to use as a mask, then open (or make active) the image into which you want to insert the mask. Now pull down the Masks menu and click New, From Image.

The host image

The mask-to-be

This is the user-defined filter created on page 137.

The host image and mask, after a filter has been applied

Editing masks

Paint Shop Pro has a special mode in which you can edit masks. This can involve:

In particular, you can use the Fill tool to apply a new fill. (See page 174 for a description of how colours influence the efficiency of masks)

- (especially with empty masks) using those tools which can be used with masks

- applying those filters and special effects which can be used with masks (see the HANDY TIPS on page 174)

- applying other editing operations (e.g. colour corrections)

Amending a mask

Pull down the Masks menu and do the following:

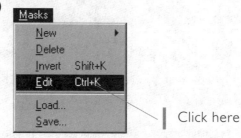

Click here

Make the necessary amendments. When you've finished, repeat step 1 to return to the host image.

Paint Shop Pro resizes masks to fit the underlying image; the process is automatic.

Here, the mask from page 177 has had the Mosaic filter applied

Reusing masks

Version 3 users cannot save or load masks directly. However, there is a work-around.

    After you've created a mask, pull down the Image menu and click Split Mask; Paint Shop Pro 3 extracts the mask into its own window:

    Save this to disk in the normal way (in any format). Ensure both the image into which you want the mask inserted, and the mask file, are open – but make the former active. Pull down the Image menu and click Add Mask. In the Add Mask Channel dialog, click the Source Window arrow; in the list, select the mask file. Click OK.

Paint Shop Pro lets you save a mask to disk, as a special file (with the suffix .MSK). You can then load it into a new image. This is a convenient way to reuse masks.

Saving a mask

Define a mask. Pull down the Masks menu and click Save. Now do the following:

| Click here. In the drop-down list, click a drive/folder combination

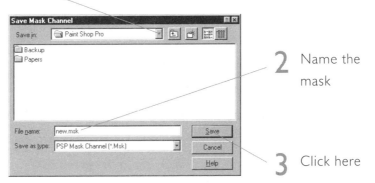

2 Name the mask

3 Click here

Loading a mask

Pull down the Masks menu and click Load. Now do the following:

| Click here. In the drop-down list, click a drive/folder combination

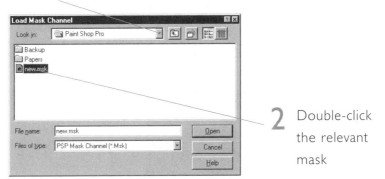

2 Double-click the relevant mask

Cropping images

To crop an image, you:

1.   define a rectangular selection as the area you want to retain

2.   tell Paint Shop Pro to discard the rest of the image

Performing a crop

Pull down the Image menu and do the following:

Click here

The examples below illustrate cropping in action:

An image with a selection area

After the crop – the area outside the selection has been discarded

Colour corrections – an overview

Paint Shop Pro lets you make various adjustments to image colour distribution. To help you decide which amendments are necessary, you can call up a special window: the Histogram viewer. Look at the illustrations below:

The original image

To open the Histogram viewer, pull down the View menu and click Histogram Window.

Spike

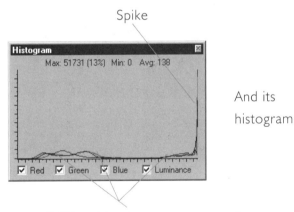

And its histogram

RGB and luminance components

In version 3, the Histogram viewer looks rather different:

Also, it only graphs brightness, not RGB values.

The Histogram window displays, along the horizontal axis, the three RGB components (Red, Green and Blue) together with Luminance. The vertical axis against which these are plotted represents each component's share of colours.

The far left of the horizontal axis represents black, the far right white. The 'spike' at the right of the histogram occurs because of the predominance of the sky in the illustration.

Histogram functions

HANDY TIP

To convert a colour image to greyscale, pull down the Colors menu and click Grey Scale.

You can carry out two histogram-based operations on images: Equalize and Stretch.

Equalize rearranges image pixels so that those around the midpoint of the relevant histogram are pushed nearer the high and low brightness levels (see page 181 for more information). The result is normally an averaging of image brightness.

HANDY TIP

To invert an image (convert its colours to their opposites), pull down the Colors menu and click Negative Image.

Stretch has somewhat the opposite effect. In images where black and white are not included in the histogram, it ensures the colours do span the full spectrum.

Applying Equalize or Stretch

If appropriate, define a selection area. Pull down the Colors menu and click Histogram Functions, Equalize or Histogram Functions, Stretch.

HANDY TIP

To carry out a variety of further colour adjustments (e.g. amend brightness/contrast and highlight/ shadow), pull down the Colors menu and click Adjust, followed by the relevant sub-option. Complete the dialog which launches, and click OK.

Before the histogram was changed

And after applying Equalize

Solarize

Paint Shop Pro has two further functions which manipulate image colours: Solarize and Posterize.

Solarize inverts (reverses) colours which are over a user-set luminance threshold.

To increase/ decrease an image's colour depth, pull down the Colors menu and click Increase Color Depth or Decrease Color Depth.
   In the sub-menu which launches, select the appropriate option. (Complete any dialog which launches.)

The original image

And after applying Solarize

Applying Solarize

If appropriate, define a selection area. Pull down the Colors menu and click Solarize. Do the following:

Enter a threshold

Re. step 1 – the permitted range is:

| 1 | maximum effect |
| 254 | minimum effect |

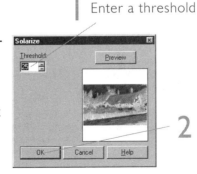

2 Click here

Posterize

Posterize lets you specify an image's brightness value; the result amounts to a special effect.

The original image

And after applying Posterize

Applying Posterize

If appropriate, define a selection area. Pull down the Colors menu and click Posterize. Do the following:

| Enter a brightness value

Re. step 1 – the permitted range is:

1 maximum effect
20 minimum effect

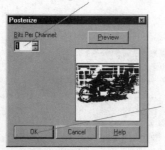

2 Click here

Batch conversion – an overview

Chapter One explored:

*   opening images

*   saving them in alternative image formats

(see pages 10 and 18-20).

In effect, this amounts to converting images from one format to another, a process which is often indispensable when you work with pictures in Paint Shop Pro. For example, it's often very useful to convert images to TIFF (Tagged Image File Format) if you need to incorporate them into page layout programs...

However, converting images singly is at best a time-consuming process. It's also an unduly laborious one, because it consists (necessarily) of the two stages shown above. Fortunately, Paint Shop Pro lets you convert *multiple* image files, in one automated operation. It calls this *Batch conversion*.

Batch conversion consists of the following stages:

1. launching the Batch Conversion dialog

2. selecting an input folder (i.e. specifying the drive/folder combination which contains the images you want to convert)

3. selecting the files to be converted

4. selecting an output format (i.e. specifying the format you want the specified files converted to)

5. optional – specifying any additional output format options (e.g. selecting a resolution)

6. specifying an output folder (i.e. the drive/folder combination where you want the converted images stored)

Using batch conversion

Converting multiple images

Pull down the File menu and do the following:

The File menu and the Batch Conversion dialog are slightly different in version 3.

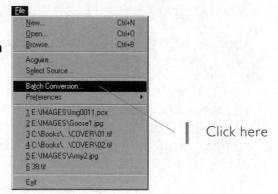

| Click here

Version 4 users can specify various additional output options – usually the resolution (dots per inch) of output files.

Click the Options button (if not greyed out); complete the File Preferences dialog, as appropriate. Click OK.

Finally, carry out step 6 to begin conversion.

2 Click here; select the input drive/folder

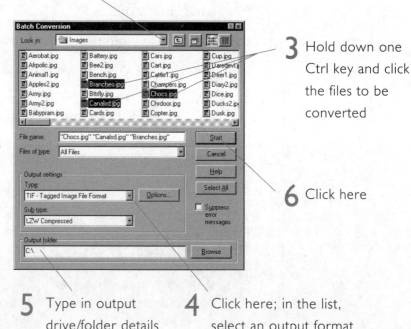

3 Hold down one Ctrl key and click the files to be converted

6 Click here

5 Type in output drive/folder details

4 Click here; in the list, select an output format

Using Print Preview

There is no Print Preview facility in version 3.

Paint Shop Pro provides a special view mode called Print Preview. This displays the active image exactly as it will look when printed. Use Print Preview as a final check just before you print your image.

You can customise the way Print Preview displays your image by zooming in or out on the active page. You can also specify page setup settings.

To specify page setup settings (e.g. margins, paper size and orientation), click this button in the toolbar:

Make the relevant amendments in the Page Setup dialog. Click OK.

Launching Print Preview
Pull down the File menu and click Print Preview. This is the result:

Print Preview toolbar

To specify page setup settings in version 3, pull down the File menu and click Page Setup. Make the relevant amendments in the Page Setup dialog. Click OK.

Zooming in and out in Print Preview
To zoom in (increase magnification), click this button:

Repeat if necessary. To zoom out, click this button:

Zoom Out

Repeat if necessary.

Printing

When you've previewed your image and it's ready to print, do the following:

Printing your work
Pull down the File menu and carry out the following steps:

| Click here

In version 3, the Print dialog is rather different. Select a print quality in the Print Quality field. Type in the number of copies required in the Copies field. To specify printer settings, click the Printer Setup button, then complete the resultant dialog. Click OK. Back in the Print dialog, click OK to begin printing.

2 Click here;
select a printer

3 Optional – click here to adjust
your printer's settings

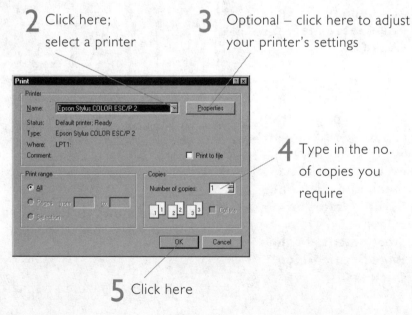

4 Type in the no.
of copies you
require

Re. step 3 – see your printer's manual for how to do this.

5 Click here

Paint Shop Pro starts printing the active document.

Index